Traveling History with Bonnie and Clyde

A Road Tripper's Guide to Gangster (and Gangster Movie) Sites in the Southwest

Robin Cole-Jett

Traveling History with Bonnie and Clyde: A Road Tripper's Guide to Gangster (and Gangster Movie) Sites in the Southwest
2nd Edition
Copyright © 2021 by Robin Cole-Jett
All rights reserved.

ISBN: 978-1-7367457-3-1

Library of Congress Control Number: 2021924234

Manufactured in the United States of America

Except as permitted under the United States Copyright Act of 1976, no part of this publication may be reproduced or distributed in any form or by any means, or stored in a data base or retrieval system, without the prior written permission of the publisher. All information has been carefully vetted but the author makes no express or implied guarantees as to the veracity of the content or conditions.

Red River Historian Press
Lewisville, TX 75077
972-353-4130

Visit Red River Historian Press at http://www.redriverhistorian.com

Publisher's Cataloging-in-Publication

Cole-Jett, Robin.
    Traveling history with Bonnie and Clyde: a road tripper's guide to gangster (and gangster movie) sites in the Southwest / by Robin Cole-Jett
      p. cm.
    Includes index and footnotes.
    LCCN: 2021924234
    ISBN: 978-1-7367457-3-1

Traveling History with Bonnie and Clyde

Table of Contents

Table of Photographs	4
Introduction to the Second Edition	7
Tribute to the Victims	8
A Historical Fascination	10
A Short History of The Barrow Gang	12
Whatever Happened To...?	66
Traveling History	70
Tour 1: The Dallas Road Trip	72
Tour 2: The Movie Road Trip	81
Tour 3: The Dallas-Fort Worth Road Trip	86
Tour 4: The Louisiana Road Trip	94
Tour 5: The North of Texas Road Trip	102
Tour 6: The Texas Road Trip	113
Tour 7: Random Bonnie and Clyde	118
Epilogue	122
Resources	124
Index	129
Notes	135

Table of Photographs

1. Geological map of Dallas, 1920, University of Texas Arlington.
2. Akard Street, Dallas Public Library.
3. West Dallas, Dallas Public Library.
4. Clyde Barrow, Dallas Public Library.
5. Sanborn Map, Dallas 1922, Library of Congress.
6. Bonnie Parker, Dallas Public Library.
7. Geological map of Dallas, 1911, University of Texas Arlington.
8. Fingerprint card, Clyde Barrow, 1928, Dallas Municipal Archives.
9. Raymond Hamilton, Dallas Public Library.
10. W.D. Jones, Dallas Public Library.
11. Bonnie Parker and Clyde Barrow, Dallas Municipal Archives.
12. Bonnie Parker and Clyde Barrow, Dallas Public Library.
13. Blanche Caldwell Barrow and Marvin "Buck" Barrow, Dallas Municipal Archives.
14. Bonnie and Clyde, Daily News (New York) May 27, 1934.
15. Wanted poster, Dallas Municipal Archives.
16. Capture and arrest after Dexter ambush, Des Moines Register, July 25, 1933.
17. Blanche Caldwell Barrow, Dallas Public Library.
18. Sanborn Map, Grand Prairie 1929, Perry Castaneda Library, University of Texas.
19. Headline, Austin American, January 17, 1934.
20. Henry Methvin, Dallas Public Library.
21. Clyde Barrow, Henry Methvin, and Raymond Hamilton, Dallas Municipal Archives.
22. Grapevine murders graphics, Fort Worth Star Telegram, April 2, 1934.
23. Headlines, Corsicana Daily Sun, Fort Worth Star Telegram, Austin American, April of 1934.
24. Headline, Waxahachie Daily Light, May 10, 1935.
25. Clyde Barrow's telegram to Dallas District Attorney, Dallas Municipal Archive.
26. Newspaper graphic of Bonnie Parker's Twelve Victims, San Francisco Examiner, June 24, 1934.
27. Ambush posse, Dallas Public Library.
28. Mt. Lebanon to Sailes road, photo by author.
29. Black Lake Bayou Road, Library of Congress.
30. Clyde Barrow and Bonnie Parker at Conger Funeral Home, Dallas Public Library.
31. Bonnie and Clyde Harboring Trial, Dallas Public Library.
32. Clyde Barrow at Conger Funeral Home, Dallas Municipal Archives.

33. Clyde Barrow funeral, Dallas Public Library.
34. Bonnie Parker at Conger Funeral Home, Dallas Municipal Archives.
35. Bonnie Parker funeral, Dallas Municipal Archives.
36. Ambushed car, Dallas Municipal Archives.
37. Bank sign in Stuart, Iowa, photo by author.
38. Barrow gas station, photo by author.
39. Eagle Ford District 79 School, photo by author.
40. U.S. 80 bridge in Grand Prairie, photo by author.
41. Streetcar turn-around in East Dallas, photo by author.
42. Bonnie Parker's headstone, photo by author.
43. Clyde Barrow and Marvin Barrow's headstone, photo by author.
44. First State Bank, Ponder, photo by author.
45. Downtown Venus, photo by author.
46. Downtown Red Oak, photo by author.
47. Downtown Pilot Point, photo by author.
48. Campus Theater, Denton, photo by author.
49. Kemp calaboose, photo by author.
50. Downtown Lancaster, photo by author.
51. Arlington Baptist College, photo by author.
52. Fort Worth Stockyards, photo by author.
53. Grapevine calaboose, photo by author.
54. Downtown Lewisville, photo by author.
55. U.S. 80 in Shreveport, photo by author.
56. Old Shreveport, photo by author.
57. Former site of Majestic Cafe, photo by author.
58. Ambush marker in 2008, photo by author.
59. Headline, Shreveport Times, May 23, 1934.
60. Ambush graphic, Fort Worth Star Telegram, May 24, 1934.
61. Floor of Conger Furniture Store in 2008, photo by author.
62. Downtown Oronogo, photo by author.
63. Hideout in Joplin, photo by author.
64. Downtown Alma, photo by author.
65. Sign in Dexter, photo by author.
66. Downtown Poteau, photo by author.
67. Route 66 original stretch, photo by author.
68. Downtown Stuart, photo by author.
69. Texas Prison Museum, photo by author.
70. Captain Joe Bird Cemetery in Huntsville, photo by author.
71. Bridge over Salt Fork of the Red River in 2004, photo by author.
72. House in Carlsbad, Carlsbad Current-Argus, April 18, 2006. Quote by Bonnie Parker's aunt, Austin American Statesman, May 24, 1934.
73. Belongings of Bonnie Parker, photo by author.
74. "Death car" in Nevada, photo by author.

75. "Death shirt" in Nevada, photo by author.

Front and Back Covers: Mount Lebanon to Sailes Road, Bienville Parish, Louisiana; "Bonnie Parker's 12 Victims" San Francisco Examiner, June 24, 1934; Bonnie Parker and Clyde Barrow, Daily News (New York, New York) May 27, 1934; "Mrs. Barrow Silent on Son" Fort Worth Star Telegram, May 13, 1934; Dead Clyde on stretcher, Daily News (New York, New York) May 27, 1934; "Bloody Trail" Austin American Statesman, January 17, 1934; "Suicide Sal" Knoxville Journal (Tennessee), May 24, 1934.

Introduction to the Second Edition

In 2008, I began Red River Historian Press by publishing my first book, Traveling History with Bonnie and Clyde: A Road Tripper's Guide to the Gangster-Era Southwest. This short, fun road tripper's companion has proved to be a mild and continued success, and I've enjoyed giving presentations, leading tours, and providing more in-depth information about criminals from the Depression-Era American Southwest whose lived geography coincides with the trajectory of the Red River.

Retracing Bonnie and Clyde has never been my main focus as a historian, however. Since 2001, the historic landscape of the Red River of the Southwest, which runs through Texas, Oklahoma, Arkansas, and Louisiana, has been the reason for my career as a writer, teacher, and developer of the website and blog, redriverhistorian.com. Along the way, I discovered that using the popularity of Bonnie & Clyde in readers' collective imaginations has allowed me to share much more of the history of the Red River Valley. This is why I figured a second, in-depth look into the Barrow Gang's exploits is warranted. Writing about Bonnie and Clyde and all the places they went to is a wonderful opportunity to explore regional history and geography as their lives essentially were an extended road trip. Fleeing from the law will forge that fate for anyone.

While subsequently, I've published more books on road trips in the region, I keep returning to Bonnie and Clyde — not because they were good people (they weren't) or because they are misunderstood (they aren't), but because their story links to a much wider history. The second edition relies on more primary sources, more comparisons between fact versus fiction, more organization, and more road trips to places where the Depression-Era landscape can still be witnessed in the wild.

I hope you enjoy this Second Edition of Traveling History with Bonnie and Clyde!

To the Victims

In history, there are always stories that go untold. Those who are downtrodden are usually not afforded the same historical place as those who stepped on them, and the conqueror leaves little room for the accounts of those he conquered. Though the nature of history has been slowly changing, most histories tend to focus on the "bad" characters: people who lived larger than life, people whose reckless disregard for others placed them into the historical record.

In this short, historical travel guide, the murderers are given far more space than those they killed. While I use Bonnie Parker and Clyde Barrow's exploits as reference, in no way do I wish to disregard the men who were murdered for no other reason except that they crossed paths with vicious people.

The famous Chicago journalist Mike Royko interviewed the children and widows of the Barrow Gang's murder victims upon the release of the 1967 movie, Bonnie and Clyde. The resulting article shed light on the reality of a violent death's aftermath. Jim Campbell, the son of Cal Campbell who was murdered in 1934, quit college when he became depressed, and he never returned. Claude Harryman's life was put on hold when he had to provide for his siblings and mother after his father, Wes Harryman, was killed for merely serving a search warrant to the Barrow Gang in Joplin, Missouri. The family had to sell their farm and find work in the WPA.

Even more tragic are the circumstances under which most of these men died. Many were farmers, not professional lawmen. They had picked up jobs as deputy sheriffs and constables to get their families through the Depression, often using their own hunting rifles as their only weapons. This was the time before Social Security, so when the main provider was killed, their families became destitute.

Following is a chronological list (by death date) of the murder victims whose deaths have been linked to the Barrow Gang, and their occupations at the time of their death.

In Memoriam

John Bucher (Hillsboro, TX, 1932) - Shopkeeper
Eugene Moore (Atoka, OK, 1932) - Police Officer
Howard Hall (Sherman, TX, 1932) - Shopkeeper/butcher
Doyle Johnson (Temple, TX, 1932) - Private Citizen
Malcolm Davis (Dallas, TX, 1933) - Sheriff's Deputy
Harry McGinnis (Joplin, MO, 1933) - Police Officer
Wes Harryman (Joplin, MO, 1933) - Police Officer
Henry Humphrey (Alma, AK, 1933) - Police Officer
Major Crowson (Huntsville, TX, 1934) - Prison Guard
E.B. Wheeler (Grapevine, TX, 1934) - Police Officer
H.D. Murphy (Grapevine, TX, 1934) - Police Officer
Cal Campbell (Commerce, OK, 1934) – Constable

A Historical Fascination

Few criminals in history have fascinated us as much as Bonnie Parker and Clyde Barrow. John Dillinger may have been Public Enemy Number One, and Jesse James may have been the all-American outlaw-anti-hero. But Bonnie and Clyde, young, in love, and desperately in trouble, have stirred our imaginations for over eighty years, and we still can't turn away from their story.

Bonnie and Clyde lived in the proverbial "hard times" — their escapades in the Southwestern and Midwestern United States skirted the edge of the Dust Bowl. Coming from poor white families, both lived in West Dallas, a neglected neighborhood that bordered on Cement City, a town founded by the Lone Star Portland Cement Company. Their situation made them true outcasts in a time when many people felt alienated from their environment and their government. In a strange way, Bonnie and Clyde embodied the "dirty thirties."

Their story also represented an era that we've only now come to appreciate. Clyde loved cars and used them as tools unlike any criminal had done before. He and Bonnie lived on the road, driving hundreds of miles in one day, perpetually on the run. They camped inside their cars, slept in people's driveways, stayed in simple road-side motels, and ate in down-home diners and cafes. In their many (stolen) cars, they fed the imagination: turning their backs on the desolation of the Depression by seeking out the wide vistas and open spaces not unlike the pioneers did two generations before them. Although they lived on borrowed time, for people who romanticize them, that time seems to have afforded them more freedom than what they could have expected had they lived normal lives.

But that, of course, is not true. Their lives were not just dangerous for themselves, it was dangerous for anyone they encountered. As self-centered young people whose interests only extended to themselves and those closest to them, they carved out a path of desolation, destruction, and degradation. They bathed in creeks, relieved themselves behind trees and bushes, wore dirty clothes, had numerous untreated injuries, lived amongst filth, and hung out with thieves, drunks and liars. Their way of life was no life at all.

The story of Bonnie and Clyde's crime spree would probably have remained regional lore had it not been for two brilliant story tellers. David Newman and Robert Benton wrote the script for the movie Bonnie and Clyde, which

Arthur Penn directed, and Warren Beatty produced and starred in. That film, historians say, ushered in the new golden age of American cinema. In 1967, when the movie was released, viewers were repelled yet amazed by the violence of Bonnie and Clyde. The film forced its audience to sympathize with the criminals. The decidedly unhappy ending jolted viewers out of complacency and into a realistic and ugly world. With good reason, Bonnie and Clyde has been considered a hallmark of American theater.

Many more reasons and explanations abound as to why there remains interest in Bonnie and Clyde. The most intriguing part of their story for anyone who likes to combine history and travel, however, is that one can still retrace many of the paths Bonnie and Clyde followed. A driving tour of their exploits leads one to forgotten roads, abandoned bridges, their gravestones, and old buildings that may whisper a story or two.

Let this guide be a travel companion along the historic path that America's most infamous lovers forged.

Chapter 1

A Short History of the Barrow Gang

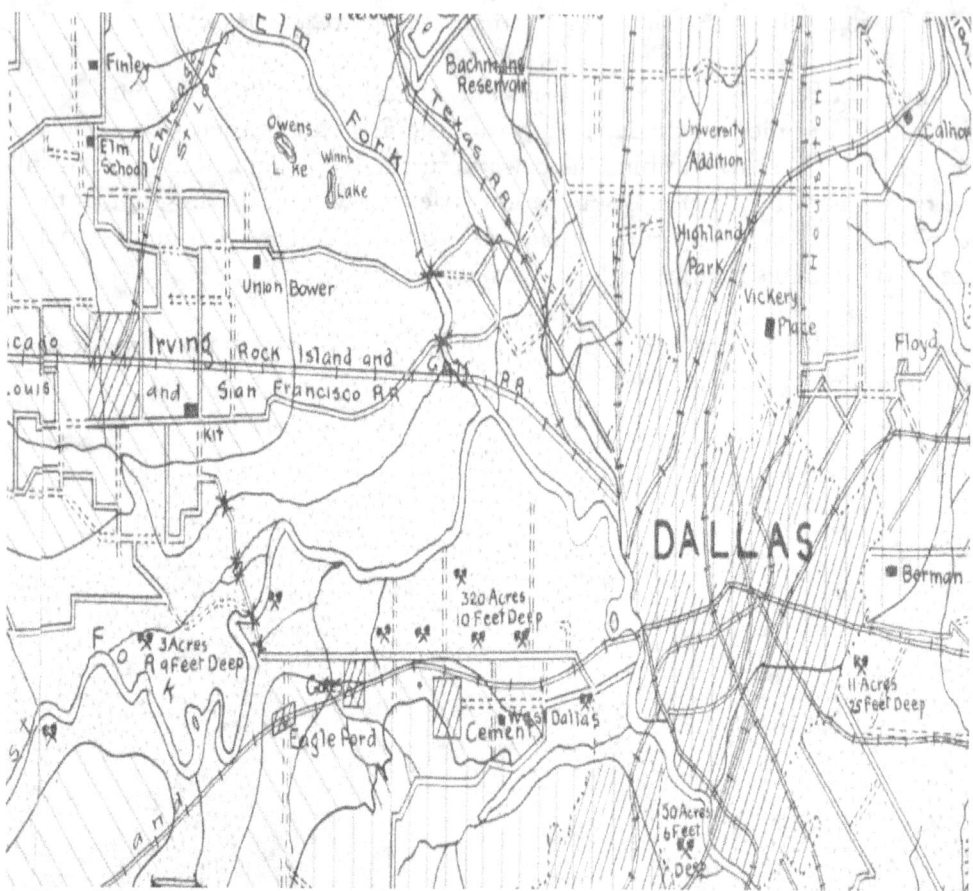

1. Founded in the 1840s, Dallas began life as a bison hide trading post on top of a high bluff on the east side of the Trinity River, which led to most of the city's growth concentrating eastward as it sat on higher ground. The Trinity River, comprised of the West and Elm Forks merging just above downtown and the East Fork entering below downtown, was prone to massive flooding. Poorer people who couldn't afford Dallas lived west of the Trinity, where the land was flat and swampy. The city reserved the area for industrial locations, creating not just a very boggy but also a very polluted place that Dallas tended to neglect. The Barrow family lived in West Dallas and the Parkers lived in Cement City (University of Texas Arlington).

Bonnie and Clyde's Dallas

In the roaring twenties, Dallas was brazenly young, eager, and prosperous. Built on business, the city worked hard to be considered sophisticated, turning its back on its western past of bison hide trading. It instead embraced a future that looked eastward for inspiration. The citizens of Dallas were very aggressive in acquiring more power and prestige: in 1872, the city convinced the Texas and Pacific Railway and the Houston and Texas Central Railway to meet on the east end of downtown, ushering the city's industrial era. In 1912, Dallas convinced the newly-created Federal Reserve Bank to open its southwestern branch in the middle of downtown, a move that secured the city as a financial center. This progressive attitude began early with people like John Neely Bryan, the area's first Anglo settler, who persuaded families to settle at the high bluff near Cedar Springs along the Trinity River even though the only building in the town at that time was Bryan's cabin.

2.Busy Akard Street in Dallas in the 1930s (Dallas Public Library).

By the 1920s, Dallas was firmly economically and racially segregated. Oak Cliff, which had been incorporated into Dallas in 1910, was a predominantly white working class town on the southwest side of the Trinity River. Little Mexico, peopled by Mexican immigrants, established itself just northwest of downtown, and Dallas' well-heeled Anglos lived along Gaston, Swiss, and Ross avenues in East Dallas. Highland Park, which would become Dallas' toniest neighborhood — some call it "the Beverly Hills of Dallas" — had been recently platted, and the Jewish enclave along Forest Avenue, where the founder of Nieman Marcus grew up, prospered, too.

African Americans lived in pocket neighborhoods to the north and east of downtown. Most of their neighborhoods abutted the many railroads that zigzagged across the city. The tracks of the Houston and Texas Central Railway and the Missouri, Kansas and Texas Railway cut swaths right through the State-Thomas freedman's town in North Dallas. Deep Ellum, located between the fairgrounds and downtown along Elm Street, was a freedman's town that was bordered to the east by the Texas and Pacific Railroad and featured an incredibly busy social life of cafes and jazz clubs, where the likes of Blind Lemon Jefferson and Bessie Smith played to appreciative audiences.

However, Dallas was also home to Klan No. 22, the largest chapter of the Ku Klux Klan in the United States. The Klan situated their headquarters was along Elm Street near Fair Park in close proximity to Deep Ellum, marking the city with obvious racial tensions.

Like many southern cities, Dallas relied on cotton as its main wealth generator. During the 1920s, oil money had begun to trickle into its economy. West Dallas especially was targeted by this modern industry. By 1918, several refineries had begun building in this neighborhood, where zoning was lax, land was cheap, and labor even cheaper.

West Dallas became home to "poor whites," a euphemism used to explain economically disadvantaged Anglos. They flocked to the city to escape the failures of sharecropping and tenant farming, and found their way to this unincorporated neighborhood, which at times was referred to as "the bog" due to its location along the Trinity River bottoms. Surrounded on the north and east by the Trinity River, to the west by a cement plant and the community of Eagle Ford, and to the south by industry along the Texas and Pacific Railway tracks (and, by 1936, a lead smelter), West Dallas had always been a sore spot for the city proper. Low, unpainted shacks lined the unpaved streets that did not have sewage systems, and residents were often flooded out of their homes by the unpredictable Trinity River. In 1906 and 1908, historic flooding swamped the neighborhood and killed several hundred people. It never fully recovered from the devastation caused by the river, which at flood stage reached 35 feet above its channel.[1] Afterwards, West Dallas became known as a residential slum area. Called the "Devil's Back Porch" in a poem written by Bonnie Parker, this neglected, unincorporated neighborhood became home to some of Texas' most notorious criminals, one of which was Clyde Barrow.[2]

This racially and economically segregated city molded criminals, artists, and businesspeople alike. An eclectic and often eccentric mix of people from all over the United Sates and the world converged on this booming city to make it one of Texas' largest and history's most interesting.

3. West Dallas became home to the Barrows and Parkers (Dallas Public Library)

The Barrows Come to Dallas

Clyde Barrow was born on March 24, 1909, the fourth of eight children, to Henry and Cumie Barrow from the unincorporated area around Telico Plains (Teleco), Ellis County. The Barrows worked as tenant farmers and sometimes farmed out their children to wealthier relatives. Clyde's sister Nell doted on him extensively, making him a bit spoiled; Clyde was an active, unruly child. He disliked school — and any other kind of structure, apparently. Though the family faced many struggles, they were close, plain spoken, and protective of their own.

Like most farmers by the early 1920s, the Barrows had had enough of eking out a living from their meager plot of land, and they moved to Dallas to start their lives anew. At first, the family lived alongside the Trinity River bottoms in a free campground beneath the Houston Street Viaduct.³ Thereafter, they lived in small shack in West Dallas along "Rural Route 6." For a short while, Clyde lived with his older sister Nell, who had married Luther Cowan. Cowan turned out to be one of the few positive influences in Clyde's life: he taught Clyde to play the saxophone. According to his sister Nell, he also lived briefly with a girlfriend named Gladys and then, with a "really bad egg" named Frank Clausse.[4]

4. Clyde Barrow, possibly somewhere in East Texas, during his short but serious crime spree (Dallas Public Library).

Along with his siblings, Clyde attended Cedar Lawn Public School on Eagle Ford in West Dallas but often played hooky.[5] Like other boys in the era, he enjoyed reading dime-store paperback books, and had a particular fascination with stories about Jesse James.[6] He quit school before he turned sixteen to work a series of entry-level jobs. He also helped his father gather scrap metal to sell along with his brothers, Leon (L.C.) and Marvin (Buck). Henry Barrow drove a mule team with scrap metal across the Trinity River bridges, which Dallasites refer to as "viaducts." Sometime before 1932, Henry Barrow's mule team was hit and killed by a car on the Houston Street Viaduct. With insurance settlement money, the Barrows opened a service station closer to downtown in West Dallas amid grocery and drug stores. Selling Texaco gas at the Star Service Station on Eagle Ford Road, Henry attached their little shack to the station to house his family.[7] The service station was not Clyde's boyhood home, though. By the time the Barrows opened the station, their son was already well into his criminal career.[8]

The Barrows' neighborhood included other families who had landed on hard times, and many of their sons also walked down the criminal path. Clyde met most of his associates in West Dallas: Raymond Hamilton, Floyd Hamilton, W.D. Jones, and Odell Chambless. Clyde didn't date within the neighborhood, though. While working at A&K Auto Top Works in Dallas in 1926, he fell in love with Eleanor Williams, who lived in the tony Forest Avenue neighborhood. Her parents seemed to have liked Clyde, and the couple were contemplating marriage. He even had her initials tattooed on his arm.[9]

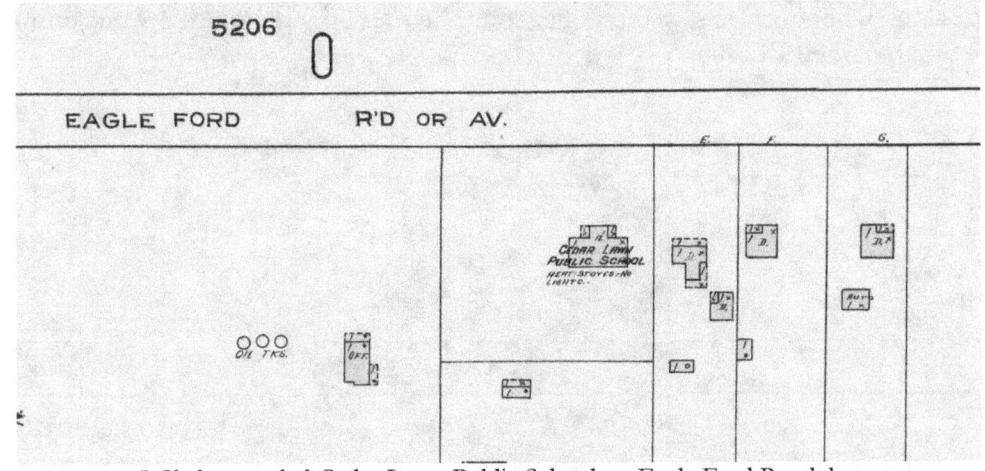

5. Clyde attended Cedar Lawn Public School on Eagle Ford Road, but not as consistently as he should have. The school building is no longer extant (1922 Sanborn Map, Library of Congress).

After a fight with Clyde, Eleanor escaped to visit family in Broaddus, a small town near San Augustine, Texas. Clyde's impatient nature got the better of him, and he rented a car to visit her. When Clyde didn't return the car on time, the agency notified the police, who discovered that Clyde had taken the car out-of-town without the agency's consent. Instead of explaining to the San Augustine County's sheriff deputy why he was in possession of the car, Clyde ran away. Eleanor's parents found that behavior just a tad suspicious and forced her to break up with Clyde.[10]

Considering Clyde's upbringing, running away from a uniformed officer may have not been so surprising. Because West Dallas was so crime ridden, police officers only patrolled in pairs. Clyde and his brothers were harassed regularly by the police, just like most of the young men from the neighborhood. Clyde had trouble keeping jobs because of this.

In 1929, Clyde and his brother Buck decided to give the police a reason to harass them. They broke into a service station in Denton and tried to lug its safe back to Dallas but caught the attention of the police before they made it out of town. While Clyde escaped by hiding beneath a house, his brother was arrested and sentenced to five years in prison. Buck's wife divorced him soon after, and Buck escaped from prison a few months later.[11] While on the lam, Blanche Caldwell became his third wife.

Clyde committed petty thefts and robberies around Waco and Henderson, Texas but remained living in the West Dallas neighborhood he knew so well, ducking whenever he saw the police, until he met up with a tiny, sprite young woman named Bonnie.

6. Bonnie Parker before she embarked on a life of crime. (Dallas Public Library).

The Parkers Come to Dallas

Born in Rowena, Runnels County, on the first of October in 1910, Bonnie was the middle child of Emma and Charles Parker. She, her parents, and her siblings, Herbert "Buster" and Billie, lived in a modest yet comfortable home in the little west Texas town where Charles Parker worked in construction.

After Charles' sudden death, Emma moved her family to her mother's house in Cement City (on maps, simply called Cement), a company-owned town on the edge of West Dallas. Here, she grew up with her brother, sister, and her cousin, Bess.[12]

Cement City was platted in 1908 by the Texas Portland Cement Company to house its workers. By the time Bonnie's family lived there, it had become an unincorporated hamlet without city services. Due to the predominant industry, the town was dusty, dirty, and choked with pollution.[13] Most of the men in Cement City had difficulty finding work, especially in the early years of the Great Depression when many construction projects had been suspended. Emma found work as a seamstress, and often put in ten-hour days while her kids ran the streets.

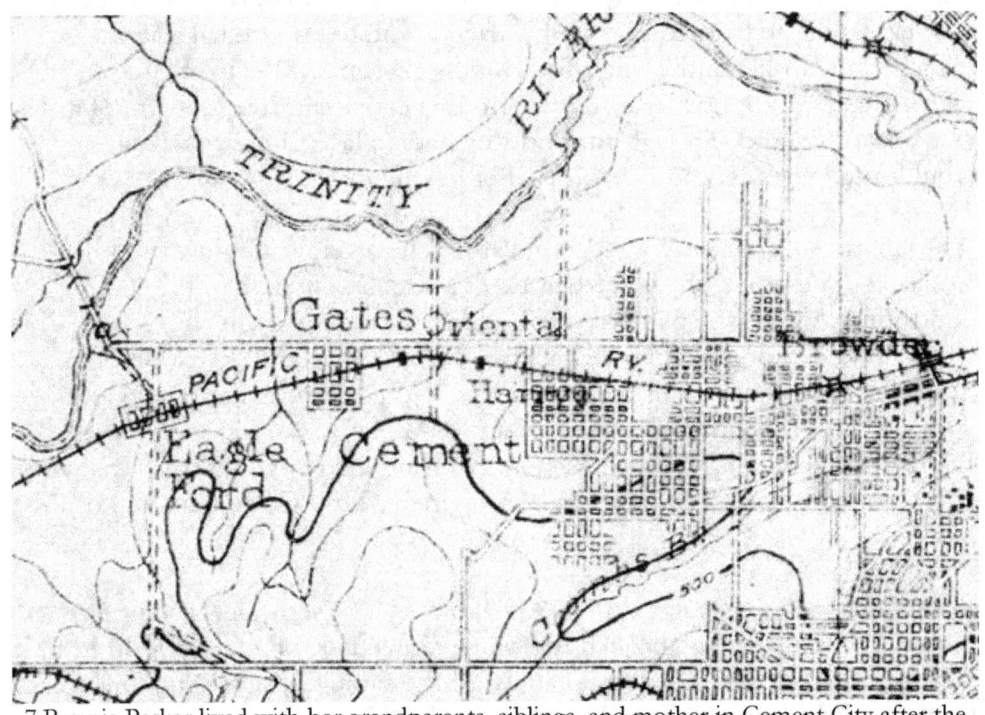

7. Bonnie Parker lived with her grandparents, siblings, and mother in Cement City after the Parkers first arrived in Dallas. Other family members also lived close by, such as her cousin Bess (University of Texas Arlington).

Unlike her future lover, Bonnie enjoyed school and her teachers enjoyed her. Bonnie and her siblings attended the Eagle Ford school along Chalk Hill Road, which by the 1920s had become part of the Dallas Independent School District.[14] Bonnie liked to be the center of attention and willingly read her poetry to anyone who'd listen. Her grades were always above average — she was considered a "star pupil."[15] People who knew her described her as very funny, self-deprecating, and a bit of a romantic.[16] She loved her mother passionately. She apparently had a big heart, especially for children, and enjoyed writing poetry. Her cousin Bess recounted that her cute looks as a tow-headed child, accompanied by her delight in being the center of attention, brought considerable attention from local politicians, who liked to advertise their folksiness by bringing her onstage.[17] According to Clyde's sister-in-law, Blanche Barrow, she later developed a drinking problem.[18]

Even in school, Bonnie tended to hang out with the tougher crowd and wouldn't back down from a fight. According to her cousin Bess, she even threatened a boy with a razor blade when she was ten years old.[19] In this group of friends, she met her husband, Roy Thornton, a small-time West Dallas hood. Bonnie was only sixteen when they married. Roy made it clear very early that he liked to be with his friends and their criminal activities more than with her and left her for months at a time.[20] Being in and out of jail while leaving her with no money, Bonnie essentially lived the life of a single, working girl. Though she and Roy had a place of their own, she would often visit her mother to ease her loneliness.

After marriage, Bonnie worked as a waitress in several cafes in downtown Dallas. At one point, she waited tables at Marcos Café next to the courthouse, where she bantered with several of the men who years later would have a hand in killing her, such as Bob Alcorn and Sheriff Smoot Schmidt.[21] Another one of these men was Ted Hinton, a sheriff's deputy who also grew up along the mean streets of West Dallas. In his memoirs, Hinton recalled being the only person that the Barrows could trust (insofar as a criminal's family can trust law enforcement) after Clyde ran afoul of the law.[22]

Bonnie stopped working around 1929. To earn a little money, she often visited a friend who had broken her arm and needed some household help. As fate would have it, Clyde paid a visit to the same house to hang out with Clarence Clay, Bonnie's friend's father.[23] When Bonnie and Clyde met, there seemed to have been an instant, intense, and mutual attraction — Clyde dumped his present girlfriend after meeting Bonnie, and Bonnie, already estranged, forgot all about being Mrs. Roy Thornton.

Clyde's Graduation to Serious Crime
Bonnie and Clyde quickly became a committed couple, and Clyde spent a lot of time at Bonnie's mother's house. It was there that in 1930, Clyde was arrested for burglary and sent to the Denton County jail. While Emma

Parker immediately pointed out to Bonnie that this was a bad sign — she probably used Roy Thornton as a perfect example of Bonnie's poor choice in men — Bonnie wouldn't hear of it. Instead, she borrowed cars or hitched rides to visit Clyde in jail. She wrote many letters to Clyde, imploring him to "do good" once he got out of prison.[24]

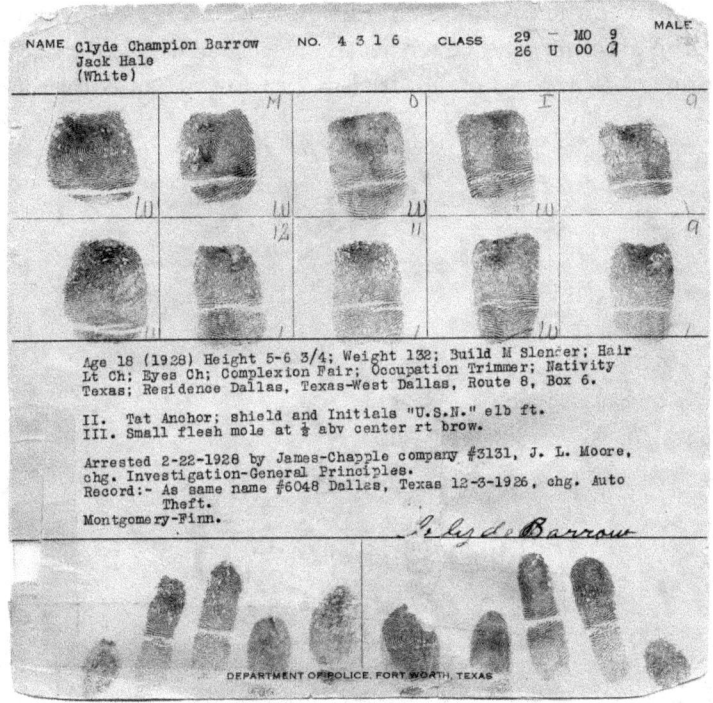

8. Clyde's fingerprint card, created in 1928 during another arrest by the Dallas Police Office (Dallas Municipal Archives).

The visits did not stop when Clyde was transferred to the McLennan County jail in Waco. During one of her visits, Clyde persuaded Bonnie to break into a fellow inmate's relative's house, where she would find a gun. He asked her to bring him the weapon so that he could spring from jail. Along with her cousin, with whom she stayed in Waco, Bonnie broke into the house, retrieved the gun, and smuggled it into Clyde's jail cell. Clyde and the inmate (as well as a third) escaped that same day. Bonnie left for Dallas and waited in vain for Clyde to call on her at her mother's house. Feeling used, her anger subsided when she received a letter from Clyde, who wrote that he was trying to find a job in Middleton, Ohio. His plan didn't work out. He was caught and sent to serve a lengthy sentence at Eastham Prison Farm near Huntsville, Texas.[25]

Huntsville was the seat of the Texas prison system and home to death row. The infamous Walls Unit, a red brick fortress which dominated the city, housed the most hardened criminals. Northeast of the Walls Unit was the notorious prison farm Eastham, where offenders planted crops, broke rock, harvested cotton, and dug irrigation ditches for area landowners. This form of "indentured servitude," for want of a better term, was a boon for the state, as it displayed the prison's self-sufficiency and Texas' "tough on crime" stance. For the prisoners, however, Eastham served as a poor man's hell on earth. Beatings, torture, and malnourishment were not uncommon.[26]

9.Raymond Hamilton liked to appear dapper (Dallas Public Library).

Clyde was among those who experienced Eastham's reputation firsthand. Beaten and possibly sodomized by a building tender named "Big Ed," Clyde struck him with a pipe and killed him. Though another inmate took the blame, the prison never investigated the matter. Clyde thus got away with his first (though probably justified) murder. While working in back-breaking labor for twelve hours a day, he met several men who would drift in and out of his gang, including Ralph Fults, Joe Palmer, and Henry Methvin.[27]

Clyde learned through the grapevine that his brother Buck was coming to the Walls Unit to turn himself in as a favor to his new wife, Blanche. Blanche Caldwell was a pretty divorcee from Oklahoma who had fallen madly in love with Buck and wanted him to start their new life together with a clean slate. Because Buck was voluntarily returning to prison (after he had escaped and been on the run for several months), he probably would not be sent to Eastham. In order for Clyde to be near his brother, Clyde would have to leave the farm. Clyde persuaded another inmate to chop off two of his toes, which would bring him to the infirmary at the Walls Unit. In the kind of tragic-comedy that defined Clyde's life, he was paroled two weeks later. His mother Cumie had been working for over a year to get his fourteen year sentence reduced, and she had succeeded.[28]

In February of 1932, Clyde returned to Dallas and immediately sought out Bonnie, who, though she had been writing him letters while he was in prison, had dated other men in the interim. Like his brother Buck did for Blanche, Clyde tried to "go straight" for Bonnie's sake. He took a number of jobs but was often harassed by the police, who either accused him of crimes or questioned him about his family and friends. Gradually, Clyde began to realize that his reputation preceded him. He couldn't keep a job, and memories of Eastham had apparently hardened him. Prior to his stiff sentence, he had been a troublemaker and a thief, but not a violent one. The never-ending labor, humiliations, and deplorable working conditions at Eastham, experienced day in and day out under the threat of gunfire, made him angry, violent, and calculating. Gang member Ralph Fults likened him to a "rattlesnake."[29]

The Barrow Gang Forms

In the spring of 1932 Clyde formed the first incarnation of the Barrow Gang. The original members included Raymond Hamilton and Ralph Fults. Raymond was a West Dallas kid who, together with his brother Floyd, stole cars and sold them for scrap. He was no stranger to jail, having been a frequent guest because he wasn't a very competent criminal. By the time he was ten, Raymond had been in trouble with the law for truancy, vagrancy, and vandalism. For all his faults, however, Raymond was not a violent man. Abandoned by his father, he doted on his mother, who experienced more than her fair share of heartache from her boys.[30]

Ralph Fults was the son of a McKinney, Texas, farmer who met Clyde at Eastham, where Ralph was incarcerated for car theft and prison breaks. Ralph was instrumental (literally) in getting Raymond to join the gang after he brought a hacksaw to Raymond's jail cell in McKinney.[31] Clyde became close friends with Ralph while in prison. According to Ralph, it was while watching Ralph get pistol whipped by guards that Clyde swore revenge on Eastham. [32]

In his book, Running with Bonnie and Clyde: The Ten Fast Years of Ralph Fults, John Neal Phillips explains that staging a raid on Eastham became Clyde's mission in life. Clyde's ultimate goal, according to Phillips, was to accumulate enough money, weapons, and men to help others break out of Eastham.

The new gang roamed haphazardly across the countryside, robbing banks and factories' payrolls, but for the most part they came up empty handed. One of their first attempts at the criminal life occurred just a block down the street from Clyde's former school: the Simms Oil Company in the 2400 block of Eagle Ford Road. Wanting to steal the company's payroll, the three men broke into the warehouse only to find the company's safe empty.[33] This was during the height of the Great Depression when banks were closing to the tune of three thousand a year.[34]

With little money and no real prospects, Raymond ended up leaving Clyde for a time. John Neal Phillips writes that Raymond left because he had heard about Clyde's plan for the prison raid and wanted no part in it. Instead, Raymond formed his own band with his brother and associates from Wichita Falls but would remain close to Clyde and accompany him on later criminal endeavors.[35] Clyde and Ralph continued to drive around, hoping to find recruits for their fledgling gang. They went as far as Amarillo to meet up with people who, they were told, were interested in joining. During the trip back to Dallas from Amarillo, Clyde committed his first of several kidnappings — in fact, Clyde would gain notoriety for his weird hostage taking. In Electra, a small town just south of Vernon, Texas, and named after a daughter of the Waggoner ranchers, Clyde and Ralph kidnapped Chief of Police James T. Taylor and A. F. McCormick, an oil and gas field agent. They stole McCormick's car and, after an eight mile ride, let their unwilling passengers go. When they ran out of gas, Clyde and Ralph commandeered W.N. Owens' car. After riding around with Owens, the pair let him out in Oklahoma.[36]

Bonnie Gets in Trouble
Bonnie had been waiting patiently on Clyde's return from his many exploits. Because she had not suffered any repercussions when she smuggled a gun into the Waco jail, Bonnie felt it was time to let her in on the crimes now, too. In April of 1932, Clyde, Ralph, and Bonnie drove to Mabank, a small town in Kaufman County, to break into the Robert H. Brock store to steal guns and ammo.

While they labored to open the door of the store, David Brennan, the Mabank Chief of Police, caught sight of the trio. He sounded the town's alarm, which brought dozens of people out of their beds. With this crowd watching, Clyde, Bonnie, and Ralph jumped into their car and careened back and forth through town, looking for an escape. As they headed down a country road, they got mired in the black mud along the Cedar Creek bottoms just north of town. Ditching the car, they jumped on mules they found in a pasture, but the animals balked. They then stole another car, but it, too, got stuck in the mud. They hid in the brush for the rest of the day, as everyone in the county, including everyone's dogs, searched for them. When they were found, Clyde fired a few shots at two police officers, then ran between them as they reloaded, leaving Bonnie and Ralph behind.[37]

Ralph and Bonnie, who called themselves Jack Sherman and Betty Thornton once apprehended, were taken to the Kemp calaboose to wait for removal to the county jail the next day. Ralph had been shot in the short altercation but did not receive any medical attention. Bonnie smoked "cigarette after cigarette," as the newspaper reported. She supposedly hissed at the many eyes watching her through the iron bars of the cinder-block hoosegow.[38]

To spare Bonnie and Clyde (even though Clyde had abandoned them), Ralph took the blame for the attempted robbery. After a stay in Wichita Falls, he was transferred to Huntsville, where he became friends with Buck Barrow.[39]

Bonnie remained in the Kaufman County jail for several weeks. Her mother, who befriended the warden's wife, probably wanted to keep her there to make her come to her senses. Cumie and Blanche Barrow also visited her.[40] While languishing in prison, Bonnie penned a poem that alarmed her mother with its graphic details and gangster-style wording: "The Story of Suicide Sal."[41]

After being no-billed by a grand jury, Bonnie returned to her mother's home in West Dallas. Bonnie felt betrayed by Clyde and told her family and friends that their relationship was over.

Murders for Real – 1932
Clyde used the time while Bonnie languished in jail very unwisely. He caught up with Raymond Hamilton again, and together with a number of men who were in and out of their gang, they committed other robberies around North Texas and established hideouts in Grand Prairie and around Lake Dallas.[42] During a robbery of a wayside store in Hillsboro, Clyde and the others met with resistance — and Ted Rogers, one of the members, shot and killed the storekeeper, John Bucher. Raymond Hamilton, still just a small-time West Dallas car thief, was pinned for the crime.[43] Clyde Barrow escaped suspicion – for now.

1932 was a bloody year for the Southwest, thanks to Clyde and his entourage. The Barrow Gang never deliberately set out to kill anyone (with one exception in 1934, according to Ralph Fults), but Clyde's temper could get the better of him, and the inexperience in the gang with weapons (and crime, of course) often caused unwarranted tragedy.

10. W.D. Jones during questioning by the Dallas police. (Dallas Public Library).

Three murders cemented Clyde's reputation as a vicious and dangerous criminal. In the parking lot of a dance hall in Stringtown, Oklahoma, Clyde, Raymond, and Everett Mulligan, a friend from West Dallas, were approached by Sheriff C.G. Maxwell and Deputy E.C. Moore, who either were investigating alleged moonshine in the car, or needed help to get their own car out of a muddy rut (accounts differ). Without warning, Clyde and Raymond shot Moore dead and severely wounded Maxwell.[44]

A few months later, either Clyde or Raymond Hamilton allegedly robbed a grocery store in Sherman, Texas, and killed the butcher, Howard Hall.[45] A car theft in Temple, Texas, resulted in the murder of Doyle Johnson, who was either shot by Clyde or the newest gang member, W.D. (William Deacon) Jones.[46]

Bonnie and Clyde

Bonnie sulked at home after her stint in jail. Although she felt betrayed by Clyde, she heeded his call as soon as he gave it and left home for good in July of 1932.[47] She lied and engaged in crime, rather than leave his side — after the murder in Stringtown, for example, she, Clyde, and Raymond hid out in at Bonnie's aunt's house in Carlsbad, New Mexico. There, they kidnapped an officer when he came to check on them. According to the officer, she asked him how he "liked being a thief," and he replied that he didn't. She countered, "You've had just twenty four hours of it now… and we get 365 days of it a year."[48]

She and Clyde formed a strong partnership and became inseparable. Clyde learned that she was the only person he could trust besides his mother, and Bonnie figured out that Clyde accepted her just as she was, as did her own mother.

Their love was strange but genuine. Bonnie was truly in love with Clyde, as her letters to him in jail show. She deferred to Clyde in all decisions and aided him when she could, making her a perfect partner. Her job during bank robberies, for example, was to drive the get-a-way car. In Oronogo, Missouri, she waited in the driver's seat in a second car while Clyde and two associates robbed the bank. During the bank robbery in Lancaster, Texas, she sat in a (stolen) car at a rendezvous point just east of town. After the robbery, Clyde and Raymond Hamilton abandoned the car used in Lancaster, climbed into Bonnie's vehicle, and they all made a clean break.

Why Bonnie remained attracted to a domineering criminal who took her away from her family, made her sleep in cars for months at a time, and put her in compromising situations, is anybody's guess. One can argue that she was an abused woman who could not leave her tormentor. On the other hand, she may have been a person who liked to live on edge, with all the excitement of danger and the promise of adventure. Her life before Clyde had held no real meaning, and she probably feared turning into her mother: old and bitter from worry and overwork. Life with Clyde offered an alternative, and she grasped it. But the explanation could also be much simpler: she was truly infatuated with Clyde and would do whatever it took to be with him and share his life.

In an interview for Playboy Magazine the year Penn's movie Bonnie and Clyde debuted, former gang member W.D. Jones recalled Bonnie as a fun-loving woman, a bit apathetic but with some genuine moments of self-inflection and self-deprecation. Blanche Barrow, Clyde's sister-in-law, described Bonnie as overly dramatic and a heavy drinker. Quite possibly

11. Bonnie Parker and Clyde Barrow next to one of their stolen cars in 1933 (Dallas Municipal Archives).

Quite possibly, Bonnie was a dreamer. She glamorized her life with Clyde in her poetry and imagined herself in the crime magazines that she enjoyed reading. To Bonnie, the dangerous life on the road may have seemed romantic. In Clyde she found a person who shared her fatalism, her background, and fed her fantasies. Whatever the chemistry, those who knew them well declared that Bonnie and Clyde had been made for each other.

For Clyde, Bonnie was the perfect life-in-crime partner. His trust in her, which she proved in Waco and in Kaufman County, convinced him of his love for her.

A rare closeness described Bonnie and Clyde's relationship. They used pet names, such as "sugar" for him and "baby" or "siss" for her. In prison letters, Clyde referred to Bonnie as his wife. Gang members treated Bonnie like a sister but were cautious never to be too rude or familiar with her, as they saw Clyde as their boss. They and their associates spoke their own slang and felt comfortable with each other.[49] Former gang and family members also mentioned that Clyde had tried to convince Bonnie to surrender numerous times, but she refused to listen. And while the movie version of their lives depicted Clyde as impotent, gang members repeatedly stated that he had no problem in the romance department.

With three murders, several robberies, and countless car thefts under his belt, Clyde — with Bonnie in tow — started to gain a reputation. He and his associates were labeled "a gang of terrorists" by wire reports.[50] People familiar to them in West Dallas either thought of them as semi-heroes or bumbling idiots. As newspapers started to report on Bonnie and Clyde, the American public became fascinated and fearful of these young kids who could outrun the law with a devil-may-care attitude. They may have epitomized the "escape" many people in the dark days of the Great Depression fantasized about.

What kept Bonnie and Clyde on the run so long was not necessarily talent. Though Clyde was a good but reckless driver, he was aided by outdated laws in which police and sheriff officers could not cross county lines, let alone state lines, to chase suspects. He drove with a police radio to monitor instant communication,[51] and he also cut telephone wires when leaving town.[52] The law enforcement officers the pair encountered were mainly under-armed, under-trained, and under-paid. Their decrepit cars and shotguns could never measure up to Clyde's penchant for driving fast, eight cylinder cars and his retooled guns. Clyde modified his guns, which he stole from National Guard Armories, by welding several ammo clips together. This resulted in increased fire power but diminished control, with the result that the bullets dispersed helter-skelter. Clyde called his invention a "scatter gun."[53]

Red Light Murder, 1933

At the beginning of 1933, Clyde, Bonnie, and W.D. Jones renewed their search for more gang members. On the night of January 6, Clyde attempted to contact Floyd Hamilton, Raymond's brother. Clyde was wanting to recruit

12. Bonnie and Clyde, armed and confident, hide out somewhere in East Texas, most likely near Barrow family members near Longview (Dallas Public Library).

Floyd to help him spring Raymond from the Hillsboro prison, where he was being held for the murder of John Bucher after his arrest in Bay City, Michigan in December.[54] Clyde knew that the West Dallas home of Lillian McBride, Floyd's and Raymond's sister, served as a meeting point for various characters of the West Dallas underworld, and he hoped to meet Floyd there.

However, Tarrant County sheriff deputies had been staking out the McBride house all day. They were hoping to catch Floyd and Odell Chambless, whom they believed had robbed the Home Bank in Grapevine. Clyde asked Maggie Farris, another Hamilton sister who lived at the McBride home with her young children, to leave a red light in the window facing the street that night. If the light was extinguished, it would be a sign that the "laws" (as the gang called them) were away from the house, and Clyde could safely enter.

The officers had other plans. They commandeered the McBride home to await Floyd and Odell Chambless. When one of the officers ordered Maggie to turn off the red light, she yelled, "Don't shoot, think of my children" as Clyde, believing he was given the "all clear," rapped on the front door. As soon as Deputy Malcolm Davis opened the door, Clyde shot him, then fled to his car where Bonnie and W.D. Jones were waiting. According to W.D. Jones, Bonnie shot at the officers with her pistol.[55] Davis died at the scene, leaving all of Dallas reeling with the thought of a Barrow murder occurring so close to home.[56]

Family Reunion

After the Davis murder, Bonnie and Clyde decided that West Dallas wasn't a safe haven anymore. Together with W.D. Jones, his newly pardoned brother Buck Barrow, and Buck's wife Blanche, they rented a garage apartment in Joplin, Missouri, hoping to lie low for a while.

Blanche was not keen on staying with her wayward brother-in-law. Together with Cumie Barrow, she had worked hard on securing a pardon for Buck and hoped to start a new, clean life with the man whom she claimed was the love of her life. Buck promised Blanche that he would visit Clyde to talk him into going straight, though he knew in reality that would be a fruitless endeavor.[57] More likely, Buck met up with Clyde to get in on the action.

Though Blanche was a preacher's daughter, she stood by her man even as she noticed he was descending back into a life of crime. In the little apartment in Joplin, she tried her hardest to get along with Bonnie and turned a blind eye when Buck went out with W.D. to steal groceries and rob area gas stations. During the few weeks the gang lived in the apartment, the women rarely ventured out, and the men used the garages below to hide their arsenal of weapons. They also parked their cars facing the garage doors in order to make a clean get-away, should the need arise.[58]

That need came rather suddenly on April thirteenth. Local police had come to execute a warrant, under the suspicion that the residents of the garage apartment on 34th Street were bootleggers.[59] Neighbors had grown weary of the secretive young men and rarely seen women and reported their strange ways to the authorities.

Clyde, W.D., and Buck quickly engaged the police in a gun battle, in which Constable Wes Harryman and Detective Harry McGinnis were killed.[60] During the chaos, Blanche ran out of the apartment after her dog, which startled the police. Apparently, she was still running at a fast pace when she was picked up by the gang after they busted out of the garage with their car and escaped the volley of gun fire.[61]

MARVIN IVAN BARROW *ALIAS* BUCK BARROW
BLANCHE CALDWELL *ALIAS* MRS. BUCK BARROW

13. A family photo of Blanche Caldwell Barrow and Marvin "Buck" Barrow was used by the Dallas Police Office for bulletin descriptions (Dallas Municipal Archives).

They did not, however, escape scrutiny. Upon searching the apartment, Joplin police found items that cemented the legend of Bonnie and Clyde. They discovered rolls of film taken by Blanche, an avid photographer. Among these photos was the famous "cigar moll" pose, in which Bonnie wielded a weapon with a cigar clenched in her teeth.

Other photos clearly depicted the pair and W.D. Jones in various ways: clowning around with guns, shooting at road signs, and proudly posing in front of their stolen cars. The police also found Buck's and Blanches' marriage certificate, Buck's pardon papers, and a tablet filled with Bonnie's poetry, most notably The Story of Suicide Sal. This well-composed poem, which Bonnie had written while jailed in Kaufman, revealed Bonnie's romanticism and fatalism.

14. One of the more notorious photographs developed from film found at the "Joplin Hideout" in 1933 (Daily News (New York), May 27 1934).

We each of us have a good "alibi"
For being down here in the "joint,"
But few of them really are justified
If you get right down to the point.

You've heard of a woman's glory
Being spent on a "downright cur,"
Still you can't always judge the story
As true, being told by her.

As long as I've stayed on this "island,"
And heard "confidence tales" from each "gal,"
Only one seemed interesting and truthful –
The story of "Suicide Sal."

Now "Sal" was a gal of rare beauty,
Though her features were coarse and tough
She never once faltered from duty
To play on the "up and up."

"Sal" told me this tale on the evening
Before she was turned out "free,"
And I'll do my best to relate it
Just as she told it to me:

I was born on a ranch in Wyoming
Not treated like Helen of Troy
I was taught that "rods were rulers"
And "ranked" as a greasy cowboy.

Then I left my old home for the city
To play in its mad dizzy whirl,
Not knowing how little of pity
It holds for a country girl.

There I fell for "the line" of a "henchman,"
A "professional killer" from "Chi,"
I couldn't help loving him madly
For him even now I would die.

One year we were desperately happy
Our "ill gotten gains" we spent free

I was taught the ways of the "underworld"
Jack was just like a "god" to me.

I got on the "F.B.A." payroll
To get the "inside lay" of the "job,"
The bank was "turning big money!"
It looked like a "cinch" for the "mob."

Eighty grand without even a "rumble" –
Jack was last with the "loot" in the door,
When the "teller" dead-aimed a revolver
From where they forced him to lie on the floor.

I knew I had only a moment –
He would surely get Jack as he ran;
So I "staged" a "big fade out" beside him
And knocked the forty-five out of his hand.

They "rapped me down big" at the station,
And informed me that I'd get the blame
For the "dramatic stunt" pulled on the "teller"
Looked to them too much like a "game."

The "police" called it a "frame-up,"
Said it was an "inside job,"
But I steadily denied any knowledge
On dealings with "underworld mobs."

The "gang" hired a couple of lawyers,
The best "fixers" in any man's town,
But it takes more than lawyers and money
When Uncle Sam starts "shaking you down."

I was charged as a "scion of gangland"
And tried for my wages of sin;
The "dirty dozen" found me guilty –
From five to fifty years in the pen.

I took the "rap" like good people,
And never one "squawk" I did make.
Jack "dropped himself" on the promise
That we make a "sensational break."

Well, to shorten a sad lengthy story,
Five years have gone over my head.
Without even so much as a letter –
At first I thought he was dead.

But not long ago I discovered
From a gal in the joint named Lyle,
That Jack and his "moll" had "got over,"
And were living in true "gangster style."

If he had returned to me sometime,
Though he hadn't a cent to give,
I'd forget all the hell he has caused me,
And love him as long as I live.

But there's no chance of his ever coming,
For he and his moll have no fears
But that I will die in this prison,
Or "flatten" this fifty years.

Tomorrow I'll be on the "outside"
And I'll "drop myself" on it today:
I'll "bump 'em" if they give me the "hotsquat,"
On this island out here in the bay…

The iron doors swung wide this morning
For a gruesome woman of waste,
Who at last had a chance to "fix it."
Murder showed in her cynical face.

Not long ago I read in the paper
That a gal on the East Side got "hot,"
And when the smoke finally retreated,
Two of gangdom were found "on the spot."

It related the colorful story
Of a "jilted gangster gal."
Two days later, a sub-gun ended
The story of "Suicide Sal."[62]

Driving into the Salt Fork

After the shootout in Missouri, the gang drove south to Ruston, Louisiana, where they stole a car and took the owner and his girlfriend hostage. Like most of their other kidnappings, they released the couple unharmed after a drive of several hundred miles. Thereafter, the group split up: Buck and Blanche stole a car in order to take a holiday to Florida, and Clyde, Bonnie, and W.D. roamed the southwest.[63] They planned to meet up in Oklahoma in a few weeks' time.

On their way to the rendezvous point in western Oklahoma, Clyde ignored a sign warning that the bridge over the Salt Fork of the Red River, just north of Wellington, Texas, had been removed and not yet replaced. Driving at top speed, his car plunged thirty feet into the river bottoms. Clyde and W.D. were thrown clear of the car, but the wreck pinned Bonnie. As W.D. picked up the guns that had been scattered everywhere after the fall, Clyde pulled Bonnie from the wreckage.[64]

The Pritchard family, who owned a nearby farm, had witnessed the entire event from their front porch. They raced to help the outlaws. Clyde carried Bonnie into the house, whose "face [was] blistered, arms [were] seared" and "her leg [was] a mass of cooked flesh," as Emma Parker would describe later.[65] Mrs. Pritchard rubbed bicarbonate of soda onto Bonnie's burns, which possibly saved her life.[66]

The farmers who had gathered at the Pritchard house after the crash quickly became distrustful of the gang. Not only did the guns make them apprehensive, but Clyde's outright refusal to bring Bonnie to a doctor seemed mighty suspicious. Pritchard's son-in-law, Alonzo Cartwright, notified the sheriff. When Clyde saw Sheriff George Corry and City Marshal Paul Hardy pull up to the house, he and W.D. shot at them, in the process shooting the fingers of one of the Pritchard's daughter, Gladys Pritchard Cartwright. They then took the law men hostage, stole the sheriff's car, and drove it to Oklahoma with Bonnie who, fading in and out of consciousness, lay across the kidnapped men's laps.[67] They met Buck and Blanche near Erick, Oklahoma. Buck tied the officers to a tree using barbed wire.[68]

The Tourist Camps
Clyde drove the gang to the Midway Tourist Camp (renamed Twin Cities Tourist Camp by 1933) in Fort Smith, Arkansas, where he hoped he could lie low and tend to Bonnie's wounds. With Bonnie, Blanche, Buck, and W.D. Jones squared away, Clyde drove to Dallas to pick up Billie, Bonnie's sister. Together with Blanche, Billie nursed Bonnie as best she could.[69] Clyde stole a doctors' bag in order to use its supplies. Some accounts maintain that

Clyde chose to hide out at Fort Smith because a doctor connected to the underworld lived in the vicinity, who may have previously treated Pretty Boy Floyd.[70]

Blanche recalled how distraught Clyde was over Bonnie's ailment, carrying her to the bathroom and tending to her himself as best he could. According to Blanche, Bonnie was a horrible patient who complained loudly and was completely ungrateful, sometimes even trying to punch her.[71] Escaping the drama inside the tourist court at Fort Smith, W.D. and Buck roamed the countryside to find money for the gang. After robbing a grocery store in Fayetteville, Arkansas, Buck shot City Marshal Henry Humphrey in a gunfight, who later died of his wounds.[72] They were also accused of assaulting a woman, though that story never panned out.[73] The gang then fled Arkansas.

15. During their stay in Fort Smith, Arkansas to help Bonnie recuperate from her burns, the Barrow Gang continued to commit crimes. According to this wanted poster issued by the Crawford County sheriff's office, Marvin "Buck" Barrow and W.D. Jones (whose name at this time was still unknown) committed the murder of Henry Humphrey, the robbery of the Alma Bank, and the rape of Mrs. Frank Rodgers. Both the bank robbery and the rape have been questioned by historians; another outlaw gang was operating in the area at the

Clyde sent Billie back to Texas by bus and, with the rest of the gang, drove west to Oklahoma, where they gathered a new stockpile of weapons at the National Guard armory in Enid. They then rented two rooms at the Red Crown Tourist Camp in Platte City, Missouri, to hide out once again.[74]

The gang immediately aroused curiosity in the little town. Blanche, under Clyde's directions, rented the rooms and bought take-out dinners, but with small change. Blanche shopped at different pharmacies, buying potent medical supplies like syringes and atropine sulphate (a secretions inhibitor) to tend to Bonnie's wounds.[75]
Yet again, there was no rest for the gang. Local law enforcement had become suspicious and, upon realizing who they were dealing with, surrounded the stand-alone cabin at the motel. In the middle of the night,

officers knocked on Buck's and Blanche's door, ordering them to come out. Blanche called out, "As soon as we get dressed," then, "The men are on the other side."[76] That's when Clyde and W.D. opened fire from the other cabin.[77]

Though a barrage of bullets rained down on the gang, they got away — even Bonnie with her wounds proved surprisingly agile. This time, however, they had collateral damage. A shot to the head gravely injured Buck. Pieces of glass rained into Blanche's eyes after a car window was shot.[78]

Clyde and W.D. drove all night listening to the rest of the gang wailing. The car must have been disastrous inside, with the smell of gunpowder, blood and medicine mingling with the pleas of both women to stop the car. Buck was delirious. His wound was large, though not instantly fatal: his skull had been cracked, but the bullet had not lodged into his head.

Dexter, Iowa
Clyde found an abandoned amusement park in Dexter, Iowa, to set up camp. They resigned themselves to living out in the open for a while, under a canopy of trees. Clyde visited the little towns of Dexter and Redfield to get supplies, careful not to be seen too often.[79] He poured hydrogen peroxide into Buck's open wound, which may have helped to prolong his life, though Emma Parker said that doctors had told her that that was "the worst thing possible."[80]

Dexter, a small farming community reeling from the Great Depression, was also a close-knit place where everyone knew each other's business. Clyde aroused suspicion just by being a stranger in town, and no doubt a dirty one, considering he hadn't had much opportunity for a good bath or a visit to the washeteria. To keep the gang from going hungry, he had to buy take-out food. In the 1930s, getting take-out required bringing the silver ware and dishes back to the restaurant, preferably clean. Since Clyde could not do that, he garnered even more scrutiny.[81]

A local farmer notified the sheriff that he had found a pile of bloody bandages that had been burned on his land, and more people began reporting strange activity in the area. Law enforcement had already been on high alert to watch out for the Barrow Gang. Newspapers around the country had reported their exploits, and they were known to be armed and extremely dangerous. The laws finally realized that knocking on doors to execute search warrants was not the best way to deal with this gang; thus, an ambush was planned on the group's campsite.

16. Photographs taken immediately after the Dexter ambush show Blanche being held by local residents and law enforcement. Buck is lying on the ground, mortally wounded (the man in overalls kneeling next to Buck's body was one of the posse members). Blanche is seen screaming at the camera, which she had mistaken for a gun (Des Moines Register, July 25 1933).

After hearing that the sheriff was going to attack the group, many of the nosier citizens came out to watch. On the morning of July 24, 1933, Bonnie was the first to notice the posse and the crowd surrounding the camp. She cried out in alarm. Clyde fired his scattergun, and the officers returned fire. W.D. was struck in the chest by a ricochet bullet, Clyde was hit in the arm, and Bonnie was shot in the belly. Bonnie, Clyde, and W.D. waded across the Raccoon River that bordered the park. After stealing a car, they managed to escape.[82]

Their quick get-a-way was probably due to Buck and Blanche's predicament. Blanche had dragged Buck, who was trying to shoot the officers, into the underbrush, then behind a log. The law enforcement officers surrounded them and continued to shoot at Buck until Blanche screamed at them to stop, "You've already killed him!"[83]

17. Blanche Caldwell Barrow after her capture at Dexfield Park in Iowa. Her husband, Marvin "Buck" Barrow, was arrested during the ambush and died shortly afterwards. Image courtesy of the Dallas Public Library.

Buck was taken to the local hospital, where he died five days later of pneumonia, with his mother by his side.[84] Locked up in the county jail, Blanche never saw Buck again. Eventually, she was convicted in Platte City, Missouri, for her role in the Red Crown Tourist Court shoot-out: ten years for harboring known criminals. She refused to speak about the gang and defiantly lied to the police to protect Clyde. But her outlaw days were over. She wrote many letters in prison, mostly to her father and to the Barrow family. After her release as an acknowledged model prisoner, she remarried a man who resembled Buck and became close friends with Bonnie's sister, Billie.[85]

On the Run
W.D. Jones left the gang as soon as he could after the Dexter shoot-out. He roamed the countryside as a migrant farm worker before being picked up and sent to prison, where he maintained that Clyde had kidnapped and drugged him, Bonnie was a willing accessory, and their life on the road was horrific. Despite his hand in killing several people, W.D. served only fifteen years in prison, no doubt because of the confessions he readily made to Dallas police.[86]

Bonnie and Clyde now lived in a hell of their own making. They knew they couldn't stop anywhere for long out of fear of being caught. Armed guards patrolled highways whenever any hint they may be in a vicinity emerged, and posses formed when rumors of their whereabouts appeared. They essentially lived out of stolen cars. They slept along roadsides or parked in strangers' driveways with one eye always open.[87] They couldn't attend Buck's funeral in West Dallas. Clyde would drive hundreds of miles in one stretch, with Bonnie drinking, sleeping, or chatting in the passenger seat. They drove randomly through Minnesota, Indiana, and other states as they continued trying to evade "the laws." Emma Parker related that Bonnie sent her letters, telling her "Mother, I'd give anything in the world if I could come home but I can't… I've gone too far." Emma recognized that "there was nothing else to do but keep driving all the time."[88] The only distraction came from visits to illegal gambling parlors, where both were known to play a mean hand of cards.

A close-call with the law also made them very wary. During a family reunion with the Barrows and the Parkers, Dallas Sheriff Smoot Schmid and his posse laid an ambush, and several family members were caught in the volley of gunfire on Sowers Road north of Grand Prairie, Texas.[89] Bonnie and Clyde successfully escaped, but both had been shot in the knees. According to some accounts, Clyde was very angry over the unwarranted attack on his and Bonnie's families, and for a time staked out Smoot and Deputy Bob Alcorn's houses in Dallas to seek revenge.[90]

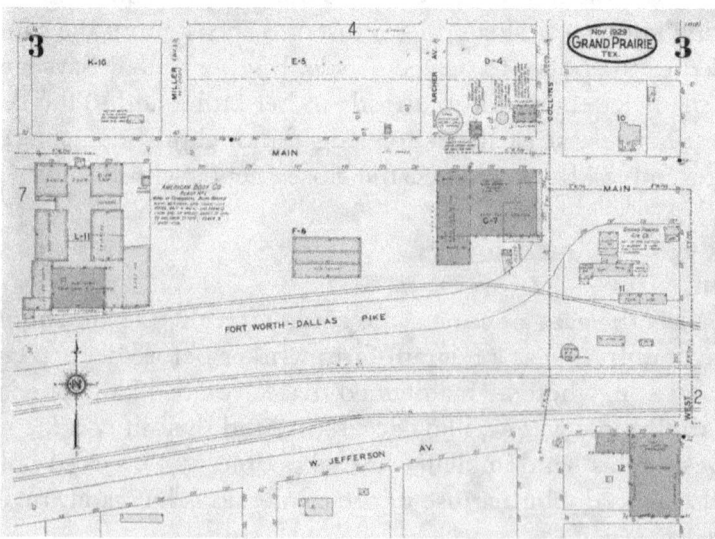

18. This fire insurance map from 1929 shows the Fort Worth – Dallas Pike, also known as Main Street, also known as U.S. 80, that traveled through Grand Prairie. The ambush happened eight miles north of the pike (Perry Castaneda Library, University of Texas).

Slowly, Bonnie and Clyde nursed themselves back to health, but a kind of fatalism overtook their actions. Both Bonnie and Clyde became even more desperate. Their next caper would be the crowning achievement of their life of crime: the raid on the Eastham Prison Farm.

The Eastham Raid

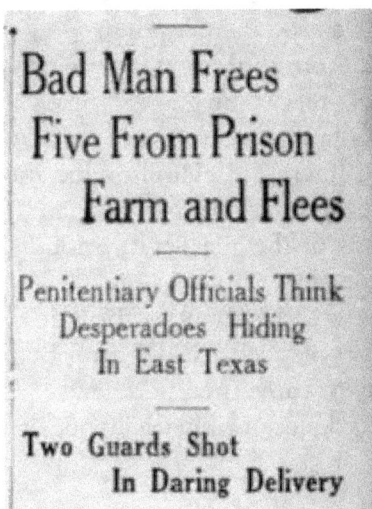
19. Headline from the Austin American, January 17, 1934.

From Raymond's brother Floyd Hamilton, Clyde learned that former gang member Raymond Hamilton needed his help in staging a break-out at Eastham Prison Farm, where he had been sentenced to over 200 years in prison. James Mullins (also spelled Mullen), a recently paroled convict whom Raymond Hamilton had promised $1,000 if he helped Floyd contact Clyde, served as the intermediary with knowledge of the work details on Eastham Farm.

Clyde was cool towards the plan at first. This may have been because, as author John Neal Phillips theorized, Raymond had left Clyde's fledgling gang in 1932 because he had wanted no part in an Eastham Raid. Clyde may have also not trusted the third man in the raid party, James Mullins, whose sole motive for the prison break was cash. However, Clyde understood that this could be a perfect opportunity to take revenge on Eastham and rebuild his gang. With Floyd Hamilton and James Mullins, Clyde and Bonnie drove to the prison farm north of Huntsville. On Sunday, Floyd visited Raymond and told him of the plan. That night, Floyd and James Mullins hid guns under a bridge in a culvert close to an area where the morning work detail would be. Fred Yost, a trusty from West Dallas, then took the guns and brought them to Raymond Hamilton and his friend, Joe Palmer.[91]

Raymond told several other inmates about the raid, most notably Henry Methvin, a man whom Clyde had befriended during his incarceration. Raymond also convinced Clyde to include Hilton Bybee in the escape plans, a convicted killer whom Raymond had befriended.[92]

The raid began in the early morning fog of January 16, 1934. Clyde, armed with either a machine gun or one of his "scatter gun" inventions, and James Mullins hid in the culvert to wait on the prison work detail. Bonnie waited in the car, composing a new poem. Her job was to sound the horn after she heard shots fired to help Clyde navigate his way back to the car in the heavy fog.

Raymond wasn't normally in the same work gang as Joe Palmer, Henry Methvin, and Hilton Bybee, but he accompanied them to their work site on this morning to be in closer proximity to the raid site. As the guards who patrolled the crew figured out what to do with Raymond, Joe Palmer quickly took out the gun hidden beneath his clothes, and Raymond Hamilton did the same. In the ensuing confusion, Palmer shot Major H. Crowson, who later died from his wounds.[93] Clyde shot over the heads of the guards. Raymond, Joe Palmer, Henry Methvin, Hilton Bybee, and an opportunist named Aubrey French then made their break. They followed the sound of Bonnie's honking and piled into the Ford V8.[94] Driving at top speeds through various dusty and bumpy fields to avoid roadblocks — with three men perched precariously in the rumble seat — Bonnie and Clyde let out Hilton Bybee and Aubrey French and then headed north to Iowa.[95]

20. Henry Methvin's mugshot prior to his stint at Eastham Prison Farm. He and his father Ivy Methvin was instrumental in the ambush that ultimately killed Clyde Barrow and Bonnie Parker (Dallas Public Library).

Hilton Bybee was later caught in Amarillo. Joe Palmer, sick with TB, was let out in Wichita, Kansas, and then made his way to Joplin, Missouri, where he would receive periodic visits from Bonnie and Clyde. Decades later, Ralph Fults suggested that before Joe left for Joplin, he and Clyde killed Wade

McNabb near Waskom, Texas. McNabb was a former accomplice who either owed them money or had threatened to turn them in.[96] In a confession to prison director Lee Simmons, Joe mentioned that Bonnie and Clyde would give him money when he needed it and Bonnie had once even bought him a suit.[97]

Raymond convinced Clyde to pick up Mary O'Dare in Wichita Falls, Texas. Mary, the wife of one of Raymond's many criminally-minded friends who was in prison at the time, dumped her lover-du-jour to ride with Raymond, Henry Methvin, Bonnie, and Clyde.

Mary O'Dare was not well liked by any in the gang, save for Raymond. Clyde called her a "washer-woman," and it was up to Bonnie to keep an eye on Mary lest she turn in the gang for reward money. Mary even suggested to Bonnie that she drug Clyde and take his money.[98]

21. Clyde, Henry Methvin, and Raymond Hamilton pose in their new clothes somewhere in the Midwest in the winter of 1934, where they robbed banks in Oklahoma and Iowa (Dallas Municipal Archives).

At first, Clyde was elated to have his good friend Raymond Hamilton back in the gang, but his excitement quickly faded. Raymond, having been a minor celebrity in prison due to his association with Clyde Barrow, had become quite cocky. After a robbery of a bank in Lancaster, Texas, Clyde accused Raymond of pocketing more than his share of the money and forced Raymond to leave the gang. Raymond and Mary then drove to Houston, and Bonnie, Clyde, and Henry Methvin continued on their own.

After the Campbell murder later in April 1934, Raymond wrote a letter to his attorney disassociating himself from Clyde, which was later posted in the Dallas Time Herald; in response, Clyde wrote a scathing letter about "yellow" Raymond to the District Attorney of Dallas, which he mailed from McKinney, Texas.[99]

Henry Methvin was a much larger man than Clyde but close to the same age. Like Clyde, he came from a poor family; his father was a some-time logger in rural Louisiana. He and Clyde became close friends, and Bonnie was like a sister to him. In the movie Bonnie and Clyde, the character C.W. Moss was a composite of W.D. Jones and Henry Methvin.

The poem that Bonnie had been composing while waiting in the car that cold January morning has become her most famous. She gave it to her mother on her last visit with her. The poem, The Story of Bonnie and Clyde, helped to ferment their legend.

>You've read the story of Jesse James--
>Of how he lived and died
>If you're still in need
>Of something to read
>Here's the story of Bonnie and Clyde.
>
>Now Bonnie and Clyde are the Barrow gang.
>I'm sure you all have read
>How they rob and steal
>And those who squeal
>Are usually found dying or dead.
>
>There's lots of untruths to these write-ups
>They're not so ruthless as that
>Their nature is raw;
>They hate the law--
>The stool pigeons, spotters, and rats.
>
>They call them cold-blooded killers
>They say they are heartless and mean
>But I say this with pride,
>That I once knew Clyde
>When he was honest and upright and clean.
>
>But the laws fooled around,
>Kept taking him down
>And locking him up in a cell,
>Till he said to me,

"I'll never be free,
So I'll meet a few of them in hell."

The road was so dimly lighted
There were no highway signs to guide
But they made up their minds
If all roads were blind,
They wouldn't give up till they died.

The road gets dimmer and dimmer
Sometimes you can hardly see
But it's fight, man to man,
And do all you can,
For they know they can never be free.

From heart-break some people have suffered
From weariness some people have died
But take it all in all,
Our troubles are small
Till we get like Bonnie and Clyde.

If a policeman is killed in Dallas,
And they have no clue or guide
If they can't find a fiend,
They just wipe their slate clean
And hang it on Bonnie and Clyde.

There's two crimes committed in America
Not accredited to the Barrow mob
They had no hand
In the kidnap demand,
Nor the Kansas City Depot job.[100]

A newsboy once said to his buddy:
"I wish old Clyde would get jumped
In these awful hard times
We'd make a few dimes
If five or six cops would get bumped."

The police haven't got the report yet,
But Clyde called me up today,
He said, "Don't start any fights--

We aren't working nights--
We're joining the NRA."

From Irving to West Dallas viaduct
Is known as the Great Divide,
Where the women are kin,
And the men are men,
And they won't "stool" on Bonnie and Clyde.

If they try to act like citizens
And rent them a nice little flat,
About the third night
They're invited to fight
By a sub-gun's rat-tat-tat.

They don't think they're too smart or desperate,
They know that the law always wins
They've been shot at before,
But they do not ignore
That death is the wages of sin.

Some day they'll go down together
They'll bury them side by side
To few it'll be grief--
To the law a relief--
But it's death for Bonnie and Clyde.

Grapevine, Texas

On Easter Sunday, April 1, 1934, Bonnie, Clyde, and Henry waited to reunite with the Barrow and Parker families for a short visit. Bonnie had a bunny rabbit with her to give to her mother.[101] Law enforcement accounts maintained that Clyde had come to the area to meet with Raymond Hamilton because at that time the police did not know that Raymond and Clyde were no longer working together.[102] According to Henry Methvin, Raymond Hamilton had plans to kill Clyde, and upon learning about this, Clyde wanted to ambush Hamilton in Grapevine.[103] Clyde parked the stolen Ford on a small hill on Dove Road outside Grapevine, Texas. Two motorcycle officers, E.B. Wheeler and H.D. Murphy, noticed the car and wanted to see if the motorists were stranded. This was H.D. Murphy's first day on motorcycle patrol.

Upon hearing the motorcycles approach their car, Clyde told Henry, "Let's take them," meaning he had wanted to kidnap the officers. Instead, Henry mistook the meaning and opened fire, and then Clyde followed suit. Both officers were killed. The gang then sped away towards northeastern Oklahoma.[104]

The murder of the two highway patrol officers touched off a firestorm in Texas. According to newspapers and the public, the Barrow Gang had turned from romantic, desperate kids to hardened, sadistic criminals. Eyewitnesses appeared, claiming they saw a woman shoot one of the prone officers twice for good measure.[105] The sheriff's office filmed a reenactment of the crime to show to movie audiences around the state. The police and the public both were so desperate for some kind of justice, Bonnie's sister Billie and Raymond's brother Floyd Hamilton were arrested for the murders. Cumie Barrow, Clyde's mother, had also been arrested and sent to jail on dubious charges. These arrests were most assuredly a ploy to lure Clyde into an ambush, or to convince Bonnie to turn against Clyde to protect her sister — because at the time of her arrest, Billie Parker Mace was dealing with the death of both of her children from an undiagnosed stomach ailment.[106]

22. The Fort Worth Star Telegram explained the shocking murders of the Grapevine highway patrolmen through illustrations and photographs (April 2, 1934).

The State Has Had Enough

Miriam "Ma" Ferguson, wife of the disgraced Governor Jim "Pa" Ferguson and the first female governor of Texas, had run her campaign on prison reform. She had already "cleaned house" in both the prison system and the Texas Rangers. With the public and law enforcement demanding Clyde Barrow's head on a platter, she took action.

Lee Simmons, the director of the Texas Prison System, had asked Governor Ferguson to issue a directive for hiring a Special Escape Investigator, whose sole mission would be to find the culprits responsible for the prison break at Eastham. After the Grapevine murders, she did just that. Though she was not a fan of ousted Texas Ranger Frank Hamer, she allowed S. G. Phares,

Chief of Texas Highway patrol, to hire him on his recommendation to organize a man-hunt and possibly, an ambush.[107]

Frank Hamer had been a Texas Ranger for decades prior to this special appointment. Well known and respected throughout the state and the law enforcement community, Hamer was tough, dependable, and singular in his pursuit for justice. Phares and Simmons believed him to be the best man to take on (or take out) Clyde Barrow. However, even a man of Hamer's stature (and swagger) could not tackle such an undertaking alone and soon a posse of well trained, levelheaded law men was formed who would hunt Clyde down with dogged determination.[108]

Well-funded and with special jurisdiction to cover the entire state, the posse included Manny Gault of the Texas Highway Patrol and Dallas County Deputy Sheriffs Bob Alcorn and Ted Hinton.[109] Bob Alcorn was especially suited for the manhunt, as he knew Clyde by sight. Ted Hinton had grown up in West Dallas and was respected well enough by the Barrow family to pay visits to them, even though the family knew he was out to arrest their son.

Frank Hamer and Manny Gault partnered up, as did Ted Hinton and Bob Alcorn. These men remained partners on this case until a warm, sunny May morning in 1934. The hunt for Clyde took them through several states and along dirt roads. Towards the end, they lived like Clyde and Bonnie did: in their cars, always on the look-out, and always, always driving.[110]

Route 66 Murder
Meanwhile, Bonnie, Clyde, and Henry had fled to Ottowa County in northeastern Oklahoma to hide out after the Grapevine murders. This mining area, a hodge-podge of jurisdictional boundaries encompassing the Cherokee, Peoria, Quapaw, Modoc, Ottawa, Shawnee, Wyandotte, and Seneca nations, had always seemed appealing to Clyde. With its gambling halls and hard-living mining folk, the region was known as a good place for outlaws to get lost.

As the gang parked on a country road off Route 66 to catch up on sleep, City Marshal Percy Boyd and Constable Cal Campbell from Commerce, Oklahoma approached the car to check up on them. As was usual for the jumpy gang, panic ensued. Clyde shot and wounded Percy Boyd, and Henry shot and killed Cal Campbell.

In their attempt to flee, Clyde got the car stuck in a ditch. Several passers-by (farmers, other motorists) stood by to watch him, while others offered assistance to the downed man. Clyde waved his gun around and commandeered some of the bystanders to help him get his car out. The scene must have played out like a bad comedy. The locals, entranced by this slow-moving get-a-way, watched with morbid fascination as Clyde frantically pulled his car out of the ditch, cursing to himself and threatening everyone within ear shot. When the gang finally got moving, Clyde had to dodge parked cars and weave around the spectators in what must have been the oddest moment of his life.[111]

23. The headlines multiplied as the manhunt for Clyde Barrow and Bonnie Parker continued (Corsicana Daily Sun, Fort Worth Star Telegram, and Austin American).

To ensure their getaway, the gang took Percy Boyd hostage. As they drove around at high speeds, Bonnie talked for a while with Boyd, telling him that despite the infamous photo of her, she didn't really smoke cigars. He also listened to the gang's grandstanding; though Clyde told him he was sorry that Cal Campbell had been killed, all three acted very cocky about their crimes. Boyd described that Barrow "acted like he owned the earth. He thinks quite a lot of himself. Bonnie is a lot like him, but she thinks quite a bit of Barrow, you can tell that... Barrow is the kingpin." He said that Bonnie was "a good looking blond, quite as cool in her actions as either Barrow or his companion" who wore a "red dress, and sat alert at all times during the ride, with a gun across her lap and clips of machine gun shells ready at her side."[112]

Boyd was released after a day's worth of driving and immediately interviewed. He recalled that the gang seemed to have no concept of what they were doing — their whole crime spree appeared like a big game to them, and they believed themselves too smart for the law.[113] Boyd also mistook Henry Methvin for Raymond Hamilton, as neither he nor anyone else in law enforcement knew of the rift between Raymond and Clyde at that time.[114]

Clyde, Henry, and Bonnie drove on to Joplin, Missouri to pick up Joe Palmer, who helped them rob a bank in Iowa. Joe then returned to Joplin, was arrested, and was sent back to Texas to stand trial for Major Crowson's murder. As the gang drove through Topeka, Kansas, Clyde stole a Ford Deluxe Sedan, newly purchased by Ruth Warren, right out of her driveway.[115]

Clyde then made a fateful decision: for a while, he, Bonnie, and Henry would hide out near Henry Methvin's family in northern Louisiana.

No One's Loving Raymond
The gang headed to Louisiana. Ten miles south of Gibsland, a small town on US 80 that sits in the middle of a dense forest, Clyde either purchased, rented, or squatted in an abandoned dogtrot house that was owned by Otis Cole. When he went somewhere, Clyde posed as a lumberjack.

Death Chair Takes Ray Hamilton and Joe Palmer

24. Raymond Hamilton and Joe Palmer were killed in the electric chair in May of 1935. (Waxahachie Daily Light, May 10 1935).

During this time, Raymond Hamilton's luck had begun to run out. He parted ways with Mary O'Dare, who not only spilled the beans to the police about Raymond's antics, but also added important information about the current members of the Barrow Gang.[116] When Raymond and a drifter friend robbed a bank in Lewisville, Texas, in April 1934, authorities quickly apprehended him in Howe, then sent him to Denton County. He made the rounds, standing trial in the various counties where he was wanted.

After Raymond's capture, Clyde sent a telegram to the Dallas district attorney, calling Raymond a "yellow punk… playing baby" and taunting him to try to talk his way out of the electric chair.[117] Clyde's "advice" notwithstanding, Raymond was given the death penalty for his role in the murders of John Bucher of Hillsboro and Major Crowson of Eastham Prison. Raymond gained even more notoriety for staging a daring escape from the Huntsville Prison's death house in 1935 with his old accomplice, Joe Palmer. However, Raymond and Joe were caught. They were quickly executed, Raymond following just a few hours after Joe's own date with destiny.

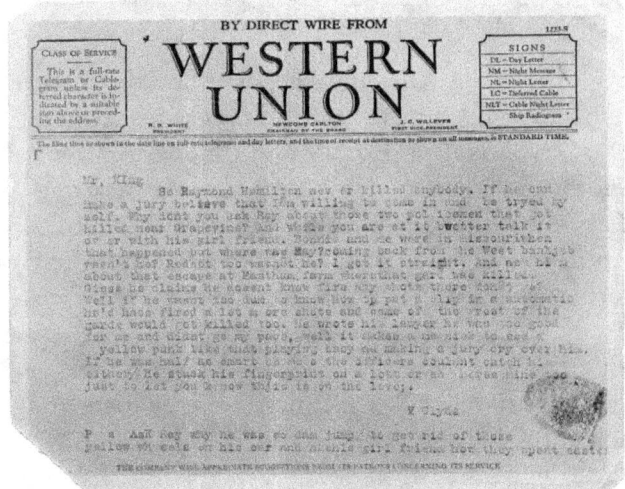

25. Clyde sent a telegram to the Dallas district attorney's office to disavow any connection with Raymond Hamilton and even accused him of killing the "two policemen that got killed near Grapevine"(Dallas Municipal Archives).

Louisiana Hide-Out

The spring of 1934 proved hot and muggy, especially in Louisiana. Life on the lam was starting to take its toll on Bonnie and Clyde. Both had aged considerably — Bonnie began wearing her hair in a bobbed perm and walked with considerable effort, and Clyde grew an occasional mustache — and both looked wearily at the camera during a May 6th meeting with extended family members along a logging road in East Texas.[118] This would be their last family reunion.[119]

They were helped by Henry Methvin's immediate family, a poor but tight-knit clan of Louisiana loggers. Suspicious of "the laws," they had been supplying Bonnie and Clyde with food and other basic comforts so that the duo could stay out of the public's eye as much as possible. Word still got out that a strange couple had set up residence in a dilapidated dogtrot not far from the little hamlet of Sailes.[120]

With the arrest of Raymond Hamilton, Frank Hamer learned that the man with Bonnie and Clyde was most likely Henry Methvin, one of the escapees from the Eastham Prison Raid. This information was confirmed by Henderson Jordan, the sheriff of Bienville Parish. The entire Texas tracking posse hurried to Louisiana. They hoped that the Methvin family would cooperate with their investigation to help them find Clyde. Or, if they were really, really lucky, maybe Clyde was hiding out in Louisiana, and they could catch him there. The Texas officers teamed up with the Bienville Sheriff's department to clear any jurisdictional hurtles.

On May 19, 1934, Bonnie, Clyde, and Henry visited downtown Shreveport. They may have been casing a place to rob or were just hanging out to get away from the backwoods heat. Bonnie and Clyde sat in the car as Henry went to wash clothes in a laundromat and pick up sandwiches at a diner. When a police car surprised them, Clyde hurriedly drove off, leaving Henry behind. Shreveport police gave chase but aborted it quickly. However, the police were pretty sure it was Clyde driving the car. Henry was not arrested.[121]

Apparently, the trio had decided that if they were ever separated, they would rendezvous back at the hideout, and on the morning of May 23, 1934, that's what Bonnie and Clyde decided to do.

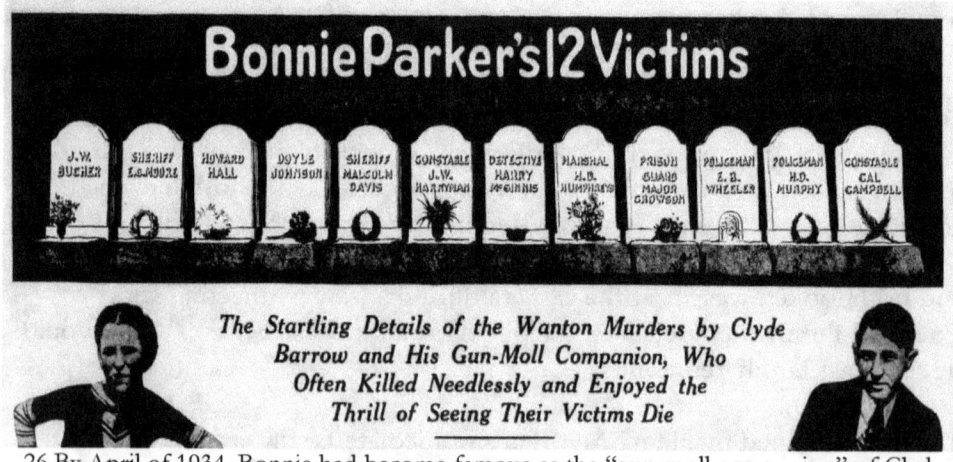

26. By April of 1934, Bonnie had become famous as the "gun-moll companion" of Clyde Barrow. Her presence during many of his crimes, and her death in the car beside him, formed both the romance and mythology surrounding these dangerous criminals. (San Francisco Examiner, June 24 1934).

Buggy Morning

Much has been written about the deadly ambush on Bonnie and Clyde. Historians agree that the Methvins had come to a bargain with the ambush posse as led by Frank Hamer: if they helped to set up Bonnie and Clyde, Henry would receive leniency from the State of Texas for the murders of Major Crowson, E.B. Wheeler, and H.D. Murphy. This plot was revealed in Henry's own testimony while on trial for the murder of Cal Campbell in Miami, Oklahoma.[122]

However, the accounts from the men who took part in the ambush offer considerably different versions as to Henry Methvin's complicity. Although Henry's role in the deaths of Bonnie and Clyde was revealed as early as 1934 in several newspaper accounts, Frank Hamer's biographers (1968) and Ted Hinton's memoirs (1979) maintained that no overt deals with the Methvins were made.[123]

According to I'm Frank Hamer: The Life of a Texas Peace Officer, Frank Hamer had kept surveillance around Bienville Parish for quite some time and knew intimate details about the criminals' routines and habits — much of this information, he related, was obtained from friends and family of the Methvins. According to a newspaper interview, Hamer believed that Clyde was set to rob the bank in Arcadia, and he was ready to set a trap (the bank robbery tip most likely came from Bienville Parish Sheriff Henderson Jordan). Armed with this knowledge, Frank Hamer planned an ambush next to a stump where newspapers, letters, notes, and other "mail" were hidden for Clyde to read. Knowing that Clyde would visit the hiding place at some point soon, he and the other officers camped out across from the stump. Here, the officers would give Bonnie and Clyde an opportunity to surrender — or for the officers to shoot.[124]

In his book Ambush, Ted Hinton described how he and fellow Dallas Sheriff's Deputy Bob Alcorn had been casing the thickets around the Methvin home for days. From the Shreveport Police, they had learned of the encounter with Clyde and Henry on May 19th, and they believed their chance to get Clyde may have finally arrived. Together with Frank Hamer, Manny Gault, Sheriff Henderson Jordon, and Deputy Prentiss Oakley, the latter two from Bienville Parish, they staked out the narrow road that led to the Methvin farm to stage an ambush from the side of the road.

Ted Hinton insisted that the posse had not made any deals with the Methvins. Instead, armed with the scant information that they may run into Clyde along the road to the Methvin house, they just chanced an encounter with Ivy Methvin's truck early in the morning of May 23. Because they supposed that Ivy Methvin hadn't gone for an early morning ride but had probably been out looking for Clyde, the posse stopped him and handcuffed him to a tree. The officers then decided to use Ivy Methvin's truck as a decoy in case Clyde should drive down the road. They took off a tire and parked the truck facing northeast.

A newspaper interview with Sheriff Henderson Jordan of Bienville Parish offered yet another version. He recalled that his own detective work led Frank Hamer to the ambush site. After an undercover officer had related that the couple were wanting to rob the First National Bank of Arcadia, Jordan invited Hamer and Alcorn to assist in their capture. Due to another tip, Jordan learned that on the morning of May 23, Bonnie and Clyde were to meet a truck on the Sailes Road and then rendezvous "at a place known as Alabama Bend near Ringgold."[125] Jordan chose a "natural barricade at the top of a little hill and secreted ourselves on the left hand side of the road and waited for the car to come by."[126]

27. The Ambush Posse consisted of (from back to front, left to right): Ted Hinton of the Dallas County Sheriff's Department, Prentice Oakley of the Bienville Parish Sheriff's Department, Manny Gault of the Texas Highway Patrol, Bob Alcorn of the Dallas County Sheriff's Department, Henderson Jordon of the Bienville Parish Sheriff's Department, and Frank Hamer of the Texas Rangers (Dallas Public Library).

Lee Simmons, head of the Texas Prison System, wrote in his memoir, Assignment Huntsville: Memoirs of a Texas Prison Official (1957) that Henry Methvin's father Ivy had approached Frank Hamer. Frank Hamer promised to show Henry leniency in sentencing if Ivy cooperated with the investigation. Ivy agreed, either with or without Henry's knowledge. On a rendezvous date set up by Henry and Clyde, Ivy would pretend his truck had broken down, which would force Clyde to stop long enough for a clear shot. This all would take place around May 23.[127]

Swollen from mosquito bites, tired, dirty, and cranky, the posse, hiding in the underbrush, felt that whether they got Clyde now or not, they were going to go home. They missed their families and decent meals. Then, on that warm, humid morning of May 23, they heard the familiar whirr of a powerful Ford V8, coming fast from the northwest.

End of the Road

The road from Mt. Lebanon was typical for rural Louisiana. It was a narrow dirt and gravel path, surrounded by thick underbrush and large pine trees. Ivy Methvin's truck was parked on a straight-a-way and was quite visible to Clyde as he crested the incline. Because Clyde recognized the Methvin's Ford Model A, he slowed down.

Earlier, Bonnie and Clyde had ordered breakfast at Canfield's Café in Gibsland. The owner of the café recalled that Barrow "appeared morose and sulky" while Parker seemed "mortified at her companion's gruffness." Both "finished their repast hurriedly and were apparently distraught and nervous during the whole time."[128] As they drove southwest to the hideout, Bonnie was eating her sandwich and studying a map. She was looking rather smart in a sequined tam hat and with an acorn broach pinned to the lapel of her red dress. Clyde drove in stocking feet — he liked to drive without shoes — with a shotgun wedged between his legs and the car door.[129] He was wearing shades to guard against the sun's glare.[130] A logging truck was approaching in the distance. The time was a little after nine in the morning.

According to a farmer driving a car behind Clyde's, he "saw a tan sedan pass me on the road, and at the top of the hill I saw a truck parked. Irvin [sic] Methvin was apparently examining the wheels as the Barrow car drew near and slowed down. I saw Methvin give the 'high sign,' as he appeared to recognized Barrow and indicted that no help was needed. This 'high sign' seemed to be the signal for all hell to pop."[131]

As Clyde slowly passed Methvin's truck, Frank Hamer and Sheriff Henderson Jordan claimed to have called out to Barrow to halt.[132] However, Deputy Prentiss Oakley recalled that no one had asked Bonnie and Clyde to surrender.[133]

The posse started shooting. The volley of bullets rocked the car so ferociously that the men thought Clyde was trying to speed away, but in his death throes, he most likely let go of the brakes.[134] Clyde was killed instantly, but Bonnie screamed as it dawned on her what was happening.

28. The road between Mt. Lebanon and Sailes in Bienville Parish, Louisiana witnessed the ambush of Bonnie and Clyde. In 1934, this road was not paved. The couple occupied a hideout just east of Sailes and along the Black Lake Bayou. The area is laced with logging roads which can only be accessed via this road. The remote and inaccessible location doomed Bonnie and Clyde, as there were no alternative routes to reach the dogtrot cabin where they had set up house (photo by author).

While the hail of bullets lasted only a few seconds, they landed squarely on their targets. Clyde was shot through the head, neck, shoulders, and even the legs. Bonnie was riddled through the side; her face became distorted by a rifle shot, which shattered her teeth, as another shot hit her from behind. Even the fingers of her right hand, which she probably had held up in her last, desperate and futile living act, had been blown off.

Along a nondescript road in the thickets of northern Louisiana, just south of Highway 80, the highway which they had driven so many times throughout their short lives, this young, brazen couple died as they had lived: in a car, on the run, and together.

29. Taken in 1940, this photograph by the Works Progress Administration depicts the road leading to Black Lake Bayou where Bonnie and Clyde were hiding out (Library of Congress).

Spectacle in Louisiana

The lawmen approached the car after the ambush and found that during the volley, the car, still in gear, had lurched forward to end up with the drivers' side wedged against an embankment. Ted Hinton opened the passenger door and caught Bonnie as she spilled out. He gently placed her back into her seat, this time leaning her against Clyde.[135] He then recorded the death scene with a 16 mm camera to use for the death inquiry and investigation that would follow. This film soon made it to the newsreels, and movie theaters remained packed for months. Everyone wanted to glimpse the demise of the most notorious gangster duo in recent American history.

Upon inspection, the posse found several automatic rifles, license plates, camping gear, food, clothes, and a saxophone in the back of the car.[136] The next task they assumed was to protect the car from the many curious who had heard the gunfire and wanted to investigate. As word got around that the infamous duo Bonnie and Clyde had been shot on the Mt. Lebanon to Sailes/Ringgold Road, it seemed like everyone came out of the woodwork to watch the macabre scene: "Bonnie Parker's head was almost shot off, and it just dangled. Barrow was badly shot up. There must have been 15 or 20 bullet holes in the windshield of the car. The sides of the car were just peppered full of holes."[137] Some misguided souls even tried to saw off Clyde's trigger finger and ears.[138]

The car, with Bonnie and Clyde still inside, was towed all the way to Arcadia, where the Conger Furniture Store doubled as a funeral parlor. As luck would have it, the wrecker (eyewitnesses say it was just another car that towed the death car) broke down in front of the school in Gibsland, and children spilled out to view the carnage for themselves. One little girl fainted from the sight of Bonnie's ruined face.[139]

Once in Arcadia, the crowd grew bigger. People pushed and shoved their way through the throngs to witness this spectacle firsthand. As the bodies were placed onto boards and moved into the store, ladies dipped their handkerchiefs in the blood that was still flowing out of the wounds; others chipped so much glass from the "death car" that the entire rear driver's side window went missing.[140] A newspaper described the car "so thorough was the riddling of the bandit and his woman companion that portions of their flesh was buried in the sides and back."[141] After Coroner J. L. Wade positively identified the couple and officially certified their deaths, their bodies were placed on exhibit at the Conger Funeral Home in downtown Arcadia.

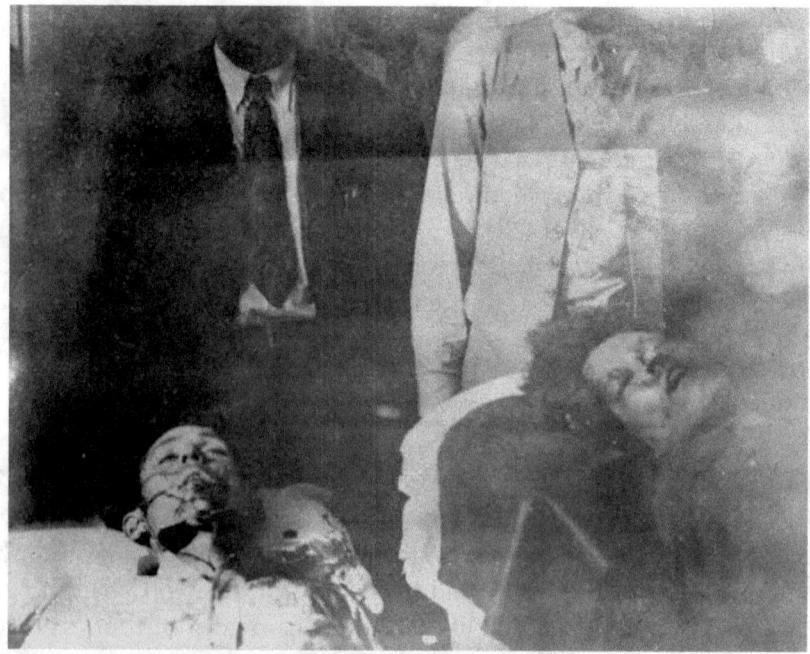

30. A gruesome scene at the Conger Furniture Store. After the staff cleaned them up, the coroner examined the bodies and found that both were slightly diseased (venereal disease) (Dallas Public Library).

Frank Hamer first contacted prison director Lee Simmons of the successful ambush, who then notified the Texas governor. Reporters from Arcadia and Shreveport quickly relayed the information to their Dallas brethren. One reporter called Emma Parker, who fainted when she heard the news.[142]

Buster Parker, Bonnie's brother, traveled to Arcadia to handle her remains. Henry Barrow was taken to Arcadia to accompany his son back home. People there remembered him as an old and frail man whose quiet weeping silenced many who believed this gruesome carnival to be the best show in town.

Funerals

Bonnie, who had asked her mother to "take her home" when she died, could not be laid out in her mother's living room. Once in Dallas, the curious came in droves to see the bodies lying in their open caskets, and their number was far too large for the families to handle. In the typical American tradition, both corpses were embalmed. Clyde's body "was torn almost into fragments" and had to be "embalmed in sections."[143] Bonnie's riddled body could not retain the embalming fluids. As she began to decay, her mother remained at vigil next to her casket; the director of the McKamy-Campbell Funeral Home on Forest Avenue, where Bonnie's remains lay, had to remove himself to the Adolphus Hotel because "the odor was awful... the entire house smelt."[144]

People stood in line for hours to catch a glimpse of the bodies. While those who visited Bonnie did so respectfully, a circus atmosphere surrounded Clyde's funeral, whose remains were on view in the Victorian neighborhood along Ross Avenue.[145]

While the services were held separately and a day apart, Reverend Clifford Andrews, an anti-death penalty advocate, officiated at both. For the public, the funerals provided cruel entertainment. Clyde's family was taunted by crowds of rowdy young men. Newspaper boys reportedly donated a large wreath to Bonnie in gratitude of the many newspapers her antics helped to sell[146] and an anonymous airplane pilot dropped a "spray of flowers" onto the gravesite.[147]

Photographers snapped away even in the most private moments of grief.[148] Bonnie's sister Billie felt so overwhelmed that she had to leave. The Parkers had been especially hard hit. Not only was Bonnie dead, but Billie had lost both of her children the previous October. She herself was still incarcerated under suspicion for the Grapevine murders.[149]

Yet another wish of Bonnie's would not be granted; she and Clyde were not buried together. Neither Cumie Barrow nor Emma Parker wanted them buried together.[150] Instead, Clyde shared a tombstone with his brother Buck at Western Heights Cemetery at the southern edge of West Dallas. Bonnie was at first interred at Fish Trap Cemetery in West Dallas next to her grandparents. In 1945, her remains were moved to Crown Hill Memorial Park just northwest of downtown, where she was laid to rest with her deceased niece, nephew, and mother, Emma, who died in 1944. Her brother is also buried in the same plot.

31. As the female defendants are led into the courthouse at the Bonnie and Clyde harboring trial, Billie Parker Mace looks directly into the camera (Dallas Public Library).

Aftermath

In 1935, twenty family members and associates stood trial at the federal courthouse in Dallas for harboring Clyde Barrow, a wanted fugitive, and the trial became one of the more sensational ones in Dallas County's history. The trial provided a plethora of information about the exploits of Bonnie and Clyde, particularly of the intricacies of the Eastham Prison Raid. Bonnie's sister Billie Parker Mace received a year in jail, and their parents, Emma Parker, Henry Barrow, and Cumie Barrow, had to serve thirty days. Associated women, such as Lillian McBride and Mary O'Dare, were also charged and sentenced. Male gang members like Floyd Hamilton, James Mullen, Odell Chambless, and W.D. Jones received up to two years for their roles in refusing to tell the law Clyde's whereabouts. Special scorn was reserved for Henry Methvin, who appeared in court in leg irons as he had been transported from Oklahoma, where he was facing a murder charge. Cumie Barrow read in a statement that, "I know that Henry Methvin put my son and Bonnie Parker on the spot and I'll do everything I can to put the laws on his tail." The only person charged but absent from the trial was Raymond Hamilton, who at that time had escaped from death row in Huntsville.[151]

In 1934, the book Fugitives allowed family members to tell their own stories, but within a few years, the furor over Bonnie and Clyde had died down. Gradually, only their families remembered things as they were, and the story of Bonnie and Clyde turned into a Texas tale. Their lives and times, shrouded in a mist of nostalgia, sensationalism, and exaggeration, became fodder for a legend that has been passed down in the state from generation to generation. That legend, encased forever in the 1967 movie that proved to be one of cinema's greatest accomplishments, is as strong today as ever. The book Fugitives was re-printed as The True Story of Bonnie and Clyde after the movie's release.

And through the haziness of legends, myths, and truths, we drive down the lonely roads, visit the forgotten buildings, and capture the haunting landscapes that retrace the steps of these infamous, outlaw lovers.

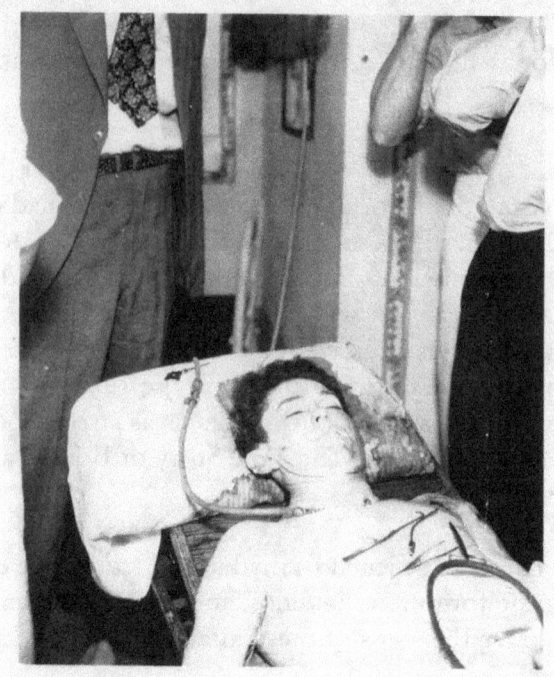

32. Clyde Barrow at the Conger Furniture Store in Arcadia, May 23, 1934 (Dallas Municipal Archives).

33. Clyde's funeral in May 1934, was the biggest event in Dallas at the time. Over 30,000 people lined themselves up along Ross Avenue, Pearl Street, and Olive Street to view the "terror of the Southwest" (Dallas Public Library).

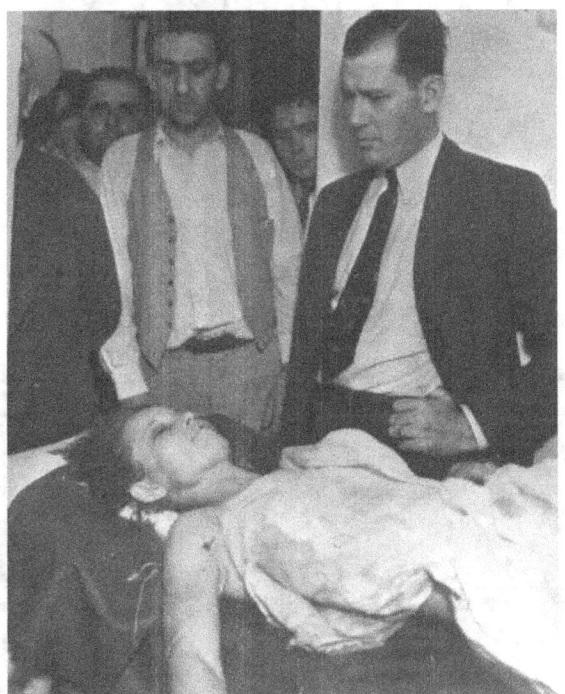

34. Bonnie Parker at the Conger Furniture Store in Arcadia, May 23, 1934 (Dallas Municipal Archives).

35. Bonnie's funeral attracted large crowds who apparently were more orderly than those who took a look at Clyde. Her funeral was held along Forest Avenue in south Dallas. The funeral director, who lived above the parlor, removed himself during the open casket showing because "the odor was awful… the entire place smelt" (Dallas Municipal Archives).

Chapter 2

Whatever happened to...?

36. The last car Clyde stole was also one of the nicest he had ever driven. He took the brand-new, 1934 Ford Fordor Deluxe sedan from the driveway belonging to Jesse and Ruth Warren of Topeka, Kansas. This was also the car he kept the longest during his roughly three-week hiding in the Louisiana bayou (Dallas Municipal Archives).

The "Death Car"
Jesse and Ruth Warren retrieved their stolen — and now ruined — Ford Sedan from Louisiana, but first they had to take the sheriff to court. The town wanted to keep the car as a tourist attraction, so Sheriff Jordan demanded $15,000 from the Warrens, but they of course won the law suit. As no one from Arcadia wanted to help them move the car, they drove it themselves, complete with its gore, to Shreveport. They then had it towed back to Topeka. Throughout the years, the Warrens rented the car to various carnival sideshows. It is now on display behind glass at Whiskey Pete's Casino in Jean, Nevada (see Tour 7).

Interestingly, eye-witnesses claimed the car's color was "sandy." The car displayed at Primm looks gray but in reality, it is taupe in color.

The Contents of the "Death Car"
Phares and Simmons told Frank Hamer that he and the other men in the ambush could pick out any items out of the car to have as "souvenirs." However, they first had to make arrangements with the Bienville Sheriff's Department, who wanted to hold onto the artillery.

Many of the guns taken from the Death Car are now on display at the Texas Rangers Museum in Waco, Texas. Other items, such as Bonnie's acorn brooch, were taken by a number of people, and from time to time these authentic Bonnie and Clyde paraphernalia surface in the collector's world. The Barrows and the Parkers both asked for the items in the car, as they maintained that the lack of a search warrant precluded any confiscation. Instead, the only things the families were able to retrieve were the clothes that the couple had been wearing.

Eastham Prison Farm and the Walls Unit
The Eastham State Prison Farm is still an active unit within the Texas Department of Corrections system, though the original dormitory building where Clyde stayed is now only a shell. A newer unit has been erected on the original grounds. The fortress-like Walls Unit still dominates downtown Huntsville. The interesting Texas Prison Museum in Huntsville displays "Old Sparky," the very electric chair on which Raymond Hamilton and Joe Palmer received their penance.

W.D. Jones
After being caught in Texas, W.D. Jones gave a lengthy deposition on his dealings with Clyde Barrow. He claimed that the gang had held him against his will, though he had been more than willing to shoot his share of victims. He served a fifteen year sentence and afterwards, moved to Houston, where he worked in various low wage jobs and took up a drug habit. Upon the release of the movie Bonnie and Clyde, he gave an informative interview with Playboy Magazine. Murdered in 1974, he is buried in Houston.

Blanche Barrow
While serving a ten year sentence (reduced to five years) as an exemplary inmate in a Missouri prison, Blanche renewed correspondence with her father, and also tried to stay in touch with the Barrows. After she was paroled, she moved back to Dallas, where she found work as a waitress. Eventually, she remarried and formed a close friendship with Bonnie's sister Billie. She also penned an insightful memoir, which was edited and released by John Neal Phillips in 2004 after her death in 1988. She is buried under her married name Frasure in Dallas, next to her third husband.

Cumie and Henry Barrow
Both Cumie and Henry had to stand trial for harboring their fugitive son in Dallas, and both received mild sentences. Living in the midst of West Dallas, where old associates and young punks harassed them, Clyde's parents knew little peace even after his death. Their station was firebombed, and in a drive-by shooting, Cumie lost one of her eyes. Hardship defined their lives: "At the time of her death, all but two of Cumie Barrow's seven children were dead or in prison."[152] Both are buried next to Clyde and Buck's grave in Western Heights Cemetery.

Emma Parker
Like Cumie Barrow, Emma had to serve thirty days in jail for harboring fugitives. Emma remained in Dallas, where she lived at various addresses. After a battle with cancer, she was buried in 1944 at the Crown Hill Cemetery in Northwest Dallas. Billie moved Bonnie's grave and those of her children to Crown Hill Cemetery in 1945 to lie together with her mother.

Billie Parker Mace

Billie was sentenced to a year in prison for harboring and aiding the fugitives. Still reeling from losing her children and sister, Billie recovered slowly, but never had more children. She lived quietly in Dallas, though she did grant interviews about her sister. She became good friends with Blanche Caldwell Barrow. She is buried in Dallas.

Roy Thornton
Bonnie's husband spent the rest of his life in and out of jail. He was killed in 1937 when he tried to escape Eastham State Prison Farm.

Henry Methvin
Despite the plea bargain with the State of Texas that he made for his role in the ambush, Henry still served ten years in an Oklahoma prison for the murder of Cal Campbell (although he was originally given the death penalty). He moved back to Louisiana and worked as a bar tender. He died after being run over by a train in 1948.

Ted Hinton
After the ambush, Ted Hinton spent more years in law enforcement, culminating in the position of a Deputy U.S. Marshal. After his service in World War II, he owned a motor lodge. His film, taken in the aftermath of the shooting, became world famous, and he authored an interesting and detailed account on his role in tracking down the gang, Ambush. He died in 1977 and is buried in Dallas. His son, Boots Hinton, co-owned the Bonnie and Clyde Museum in Gibsland, Louisiana.

Frank Hamer
A lifelong Texas Ranger, Frank Hamer received a special congressional citation for his role in tracking Bonnie and Clyde. After the ambush, he became a special agent for the Texas Rangers, being recalled on occasion to bust strikes, maintain order in dangerous situations, and supervise contested elections. He died in his sleep in 1955 and is buried in Austin. His life was recounted by H. Gordon Frost and John Holmes Jenkins in the 1968 book, I'm Frank Hamer.

The Victims
No one who goes on a journey to discover the history of Bonnie and Clyde should forget that the victims of their crimes were not just those who died.

The families they left behind told of economic and psychological hardships, as their main breadwinners and heads of household were killed during one of America's worst depressions. Without their fathers, children had to leave school to earn money to keep the family farms afloat. Women who were widowed with young children had to seek work wherever they could find it. These murders occurred in the era before Social Security (though FDR implemented the system by the late 1930s), and many of the victims' families became destitute. The Barrow Gang wrecked more havoc than they could have ever imagined.

Chapter 3

Traveling History

37. Stuart, Iowa is right proud of their connection to the Barrow Gang (photo by author).

Discovering Depression-era sights in the Southwest is exciting enough. Coupled with a notorious history, traveling can be even more rewarding. With an itinerary in one hand, this book in another, and an active imagination, a road tripper is able to "place" the actual stories. Photos only do a small amount of justice — understanding and reliving history by exploration is not only more informative, but also a lot more fun.

"Traveling History of Bonnie and Clyde" takes the reader all over the Southwest, and even beyond. These trips can be taken in short spurts, in one long road trip that may take three days or more, or just through proximity if travelers happen to find themselves near a site. Meandering along stretches of roads that Clyde Barrow raced down, driving through towns that witnessed the hardships of the Depression, and winding through the lesser-known streets of Dallas provides an intimate feel of the real history of the Gangster-era. Locations from the 1967 movie have also been included in a separate tour, as this iconic film changed the entire crime-genre in American cinema and launched the storied careers of Warren Beatty, Faye Dunaway, Gene Wilder, Michael Pollard, and Estelle Parsons.

Tour 1 — The Dallas Road Trip

Bonnie and Clyde lived and loved in Dallas, and it seemed that they also loved their city. This is why Dallas can be considered the gang's third and constant member. The couple continuously returned to the city to visit their families, each time at high risk to themselves and others. West Dallas specifically provides the couple's immediate history — newspaper reporters in the 1930s called this area a "Little Cicero" and, while the shot-gun houses are mostly gone, West Dallas is still a little on the dilapidated side. This tour encompasses the entire city, however; North Dallas, East Dallas, Oak Cliff, the Devil's Back Porch, and downtown are all part of the trip.

The tour will explain which places may be "drive-by" only (meaning, no or limited stopping/parking ability, mainly because the site is located on private property), an "opportunity to stop," or a "definite stop." All driving, parking, and visiting is done at the reader's own risk.

But beware; Dallas is re-inventing itself once again, and one of the targeted redevelopment areas is West Dallas, where the first few sites of the tour are located. So go out there and see these places before development takes over!

West Dallas Neighborhood
Barrow Star Service Station
Fish Trap Cemetery
Cement City Elementary School
West Dallas Viaduct
Crown Hill Memorial Park
Swiss Avenue Circle Street Car Stop
Belo Mansion/ Dallas Bar Association (Sparkman Holtz Funeral Home)
U.S. Federal Courthouse
Dallas County Jail
Dallas County Courthouse
Emma Parker's Home
Western Heights Cemetery

Site of Malcolm Davis's murder in 1932 (private property; drive-by only)

Location: 3111 North Winnetka Avenue, Dallas.
Coordinates: 32.7798936, -96.8421252
What's to see: When crossing the Trinity River from downtown into West Dallas, the traveler now drives on the Margaret Hunt Hill Bridge at Singleton Boulevard. Built in 2007 by the famous architect, Santiago Calavtrava, this beautiful structure replaced a concrete bridge from the 1920s, which is now a pedestrian thoroughfare to its north.

Singleton Boulevard anchors West Dallas; during Bonnie and Clyde's time, this was known as Eagle Ford Road as it led to the little hamlet of Eagle Ford along the Trinity River and the Texas & Pacific Railway.

Many of Clyde's associates lived along Eagle Ford Road, now Singleton Boulevard, chief among them the Hamilton family. Raymond's mother's house sits at the left (west) corner of Singleton Boulevard and Winnetka Avenue. At the 3100 block of Winnetka Avenue is the home once occupied by Lillian McBride, sister to gang member Raymond Hamilton (in 1932, the address was 507 County Avenue). Clyde shot and killed Dallas County Deputy Sheriff Malcolm Davis next to the fort porch. The house is now owned by the Wesley Rankin Center, a non-profit community organization, that is working with the city to provide it landmark status.

Barrow "Star" Service Station (private property but potential stop; limited parking)

Location: 1221 Singleton Boulevard, Dallas.
Coordinates: 32.778733, -96.8434523
What's to see: Henry and Cumie Barrow sold Texaco gas from two pumps, as well as cold drinks and snacks. The Barrow family lived in two rooms attached to the gas station. From where Henry Barrow pumped gas, he commanded a great view of the Dallas skyline. The service station was built from wood, but throughout the years it has been bricked, painted, then painted again, so there's not much of the original building left. The Barrows operated the service station in the early years of the 1930s, after Clyde was already a known criminal.

38. The gas station in 2004, where Henry and Cumie Barrow, Clyde's parents, once sold Texaco gas and cold drinks (photo by author).

Fish Trap Cemetery, also known as the La Reunion Cemetery (definite stop)
Location: Fish Trap Road (no address), Singleton Boulevard, Dallas.
Coordinates: 32.7834432, -96.862669What's to see: Bonnie was first buried at Fish Trap Cemetery, once known as the La Reunion Cemetery, though her grave was moved to Crown Hill Memorial Park close to Love Field in the 1940s. Her grandparents, Frank and Mary Krause, remain buried here — their tombstones are located along the south fence line that can be seen outside of the fence if the cemetery is not open. Another relative, a soldier who died during the Great War, is also buried in the family plot.

La Reunion Cemetery is also the last home of many "La Reunion" settlers. La Reunion was an experiment by Swiss, French, and Belgian immigrants who, in the 1850s, wanted to create a socialist community around the Trinity River. That didn't work, and their descendents went on to become the workers and civic leaders of burgeoning Dallas.

Bonnie's Grade School in Cement City (private property but potential stop; do not park in lot)
Location: 1601 Chalk Hill Road, Dallas.
Coordinates: 32.7635253, -96.9048842
What's to see: The old West Dallas school building, which Bonnie attended until eighth grade, is now restored and home to a private event business. The school was built from concrete made at the cement plant and served the children of the plant workers as well as others in West Dallas. The school is emblazoned as "Eagle Ford District No. 79," meaning it was the 79th school

built in Dallas County and was located at the now-ghost town of Eagle Ford. It has been designated a Dallas Historical Landmark.

39. Bonnie shined as a student at the Eagle Ford District No. 79 School, which also served the children in Cement City. The building is now a City of Dallas Historical Landmark. In 2021, it is occupied by an event company (photo by author).

Cement City was a loose collection of company housing surrounding the cement plant located just east of Chalk Hill Road.

Neither Clyde nor any of the Barrow siblings attended this school. Instead, they attended the Cedar Lawn School on Eagle Ford Road, which stood across from their family's future gas station on Eagle Ford Road/ Singleton Boulevard. This building no longer stands.

West Dallas Viaduct (definite stop)
Location: 2000 E Shady Grove Road, Irving.
Coordinates: 32.7991336, -96.9195299
What's to see: Prior to the construction of Interstate 30, Eagle Ford Road turned northward after Chalk Hill Road and crossed the Trinity River in a series of bridges, all built in the 1920s from concrete manufactured in Cement City. This road eventually led the traveler to Irving and Grapevine. Today, these bridges have been decommissioned but still can be enjoyed as a pedestrian trail.

Now called the Campion Trail, this old roadbed is part of a series of roads that led western Dallas to Irving and Grapevine in Gangster-Era Dallas. At the beginning of the trail is one of the roads' bridges, built in the 1920s using Portland Cement manufactured at Cement City. Along this road, the

Barrows and Parkers would meet up with Bonnie and Clyde for their family reunions. The road is what Bonnie labeled the entrance to the "Devil's Back Porch:"

> From Irving to the West Dallas Viaduct
> Is known as the Great Divide
> Where women are kin, and men are men
> And no one stools on Bonnie and Clyde.

40. A series of bridges linked the Fort Worth Pike with Sowers Road, where the ambush with the Dallas Sheriff's Office occurred in November 1933. The bridges still stand but have been replaced by modern structures on U.S. 180. However, some of the bridges on the east side of the Trinity River can still be traversed as they've been converted to a walking/ biking trail (photo by author).

41. Bonnie once worked at a café at a streetcar turn-around. She took the streetcar to work, as she lived with her mother in a small house where now the Winspear Opera House and Meyerson Symphony Center stand. After Bonnie stopped working at the café, she met Clyde (photo by author).

Swiss Circle Streetcar Stop (stopping opportunity)
Location: 3308 Swiss Circle, Dallas.
Coordinates: 32.7907111, -96.7847384
What's to see: In 1929, Bonnie worked as a waitress at Hargrave's Café at the Swiss Circle streetcar stop. Bonnie took the streetcar back and forth to work from her mother's house, which stood at 1909 Crockett Street.[153]

Belo Mansion/ Dallas Bar Association (private property; drive-by only)
Location: 2101 Ross Avenue, Dallas.
Coordinates: 32.788352, -96.8008266
What's to See: Clyde Barrow's embalming and funeral took place at the Sparkman-Holtz Funeral Home, once the home of the Belos, publisher of the Dallas Morning News. Ross Avenue was once lined with prominent architecture like the Belo Mansion. Today, the mansion, the last of its kind on Ross Avenue, is home to the Dallas Bar Association.

U.S. Federal Courthouse (potential stopping opportunity; limited parking)
Location: 400 N. Ervay, Dallas.
Coordinates: 32.783848, -96.8005366
What's to see: The federal courthouse, which also houses a post office, has been converted into apartments. Built in the typical federalist style of the 1920s, this is the location of the Clyde Barrow Harboring Trial of February 1935, where twenty associates, including Clyde and Bonnie's mothers, were

convicted of aiding and abetting Bonnie Parker and Clyde Barrow. The newspaper called this trial the largest organized crime conviction in the Southwest.

Dallas County Criminal Courts and "Old Red" Dallas County Courthouse (stopping opportunity)
Location: 100 S. Houston Street, Dallas.
Coordinates: 32.7786585, -96.809616
What's to see: The Criminal Courts Building housed the county jail from which Raymond Hamilton once escaped. The courthouse, now the Old Red Courthouse Museum, acted as the city's central courthouse during Gangster-Era Dallas; this is where Bonnie Parker married Roy Thornton. Both buildings face Dealey Plaza, site of the assassination of President John F. Kennedy in 1963. Jack Ruby's trial for shooting Lee Harvey Oswald took place inside the Criminal Courts building.

Houston Street Viaduct (drive-by only)
Location: Houston Street over the Trinity River, Dallas.
Coordinates: 32.772227, -96.8092317
What's to see: The Houston Street Viaduct, built of Portland Cement manufactured in Cement City, was erected in 1911 after an earlier bridge was damaged due to a massive flood in 1908. Beneath this bridge was a free campground during the 1920s; this is where the Barrows lived when they first came to Dallas. Henry Barrow's mule cart was destroyed by an automobile on this bridge, too.

Emma Parker's Home (private property; drive-by only)
Location: 232 W Eighth Street, Dallas.
Coordinates: 32.7478218, -96.828182
What's to see: As a renter who needed to save money, Emma Parker moved at least once per year, sometimes more, to avoid inevitable rent hikes. Almost all of her homes, and the entire neighborhoods surrounding them, have since been demolished. While the FBI's wanted poster from 1934 listed her address at 1216 S. Lamar Street, the Dallas City Directory from 1934 lists her address as 232 W. Eighth Street. This is the home where she learned that Bonnie had been killed in the ambush in Louisiana.

Crown Hill Memorial Park (definite stop)
Location: 9700 Webb Chapel Road, Dallas.
Coordinates: 32.8659917, -96.864973
What's to see: Bonnie Parker is buried in the center of Crown Hill Memorial Park after having been moved from Fish Trap Cemetery by her sister, Billie

Parker Mace. Near her grave also rest her niece and nephew, both of whom died within days of each other; her brother, Buster (who accompanied her body to Dallas after the 1934 ambush); and her mother, Emma Parker.

To find Bonnie's grave, park on the left (west) side of the mausoleum. Follow the tall hedgerow on the west side to approximately the middle (the grave is next to an upright tombstone labeled "Tyner.") Bonnie's grave will be nestled against the hedgerow near cedar trees on the western side of the hedges. Her epitaph reads:

> AS THE FLOWERS ARE ALL MADE SWEETER BY
> THE SUNSHINE AND THE DEW,
> SO THIS OLD WORLD IS MADE BRIGHTER BY
> THE LIVES OF FOLKS LIKE YOU.

The bronze-cast tombstone is encased in concrete to deter theft. The verse is part of a poem Bonnie composed. The plaque itself was an anonymous purchase, purportedly by a funeral director whom Bonnie and Clyde paid in preparation of their funerals. However, the Parker and Barrow families had wisely purchased their own burial policies for their wayward children. The money paid by Bonnie and Clyde to the funeral director, who did not share his name due to potential legal ramifications of in aiding and abetting fugitives, was then directed to pay for Bonnie's plaque.

42. Near Bonnie's grave lie her niece, nephew, brother, and her mother, Emma (photo by author).

Western Heights Cemetery (definite stop)
Location: 1617 Fort Worth Avenue, Dallas.
Coordinates: 32.7656281, -96.8483812
What's to see: A small cemetery with many immigrant graves, the Barrow family plot lies along a fence row on the west side. The surviving Barrow family maintains the graveyard and even placed a bricked footpath to help visitors find the graves. The cemetery was once off-limits to visitors but due to continued interest, the forbidding chain link fence was replaced with an inviting iron gate.

Clyde shares a tombstone with his brother, Marvin "Buck" Barrow. When Buck died in July of 1933, the family first placed a simple marker, "M I B," to indicate where the man was buried; the actual tombstone was completed once Clyde met his inevitable demise.

In the 1980s, a politician from Oklahoma City stole the upright tombstone during a drunken night after the annual University of Texas v. University of Oklahoma football game. Upon retrieval, the Barrow family placed the tombstone horizontally and in concrete to prevent future destruction.

43. The final respites of Henry and Cumie Barrow and Elvin Barrow, a brother, lie near the grave for Clyde and Marvin "Buck" Barrow (photo by author).

Tour 2 — The Movie Road Trip

In 1967, Arthur Penn and Warren Beatty directed and produced a movie unlike any that had been seen before. "Bonnie and Clyde" was not the classic gangster movie of Old Hollywood; the film sympathized with the criminals and dared the audience to do the same. The brutal and gory ending of a movie that ran the gamut of emotions was meant to shock and provoke, creating a new genre in modern American filmmaking in the process. It also introduced a new generation to Clyde Barrow and Bonnie Parker. Without the movie, these "desperados of the Southwest" might not have held the interest for so many decades afterwards.

To any student of Bonnie and Clyde's history, however, the creative licenses taken by the film are obvious. While the movie stayed true to the relative timeline, it had to sacrifice some accuracy for clarity's sake. Clyde met Bonnie not while trying to steal her mother's car, but at a mutual friend's house — and because they ran in the same circles in the same West Dallas neighborhood, they were probably keenly aware of each other already. While the film portrays Clyde as impotent, he reportedly had no such trouble with Bonnie; the fact that she was never pregnant may have been due to dangerous birth control practices.[154] Frank Hamer, the famed Texas Ranger, was not hell-bent on personal revenge against the pair, and when the posse ambushed them, Clyde never left the car. Blanche Barrow never revealed anything to Frank Hamer, as she had already been arrested and jailed before the lawman became involved. Lastly, the most blatant substitution is the fictional character "C.W. Moss," the gang's third member, played by Michael Pollard. Moss is an amalgamation of Raymond Hamilton, Ralph Fults, W.D. Jones, and Henry Methvin.

The filmmakers stayed true to the general locations, however. They shot the film in and around Dallas, seeking and finding places that looked and felt like the 1930s. Taking a drive to the movie locations in Dallas, Ellis, and Denton counties is a fun adventure that uses the same old roads that Bonnie Parker, Clyde Barrow, Faye Dunaway, and Warren Beatty traveled, albeit thirty years apart.[155]

In 2018, the movie "The Highwaymen," starring Kevin Costner and Woody Harrelson, debuted to much fanfare. Focusing on the law's side of the ambush, the film's timeline is fairly accurate, though the personal stories (such as Manny Gault's degraded state, or Bonnie shooting the Grapevine police officers) are not. Much of the filming took place in southern

Louisiana, with the ambush depicted along the same road where the actual historical event occurred.

This tour focuses on the locations of the ground-breaking 1967 movie.

> Ponder, Texas
> Venus, Texas
> Maypearl, Texas
> Red Oak, Texas
> Pilot Point, Texas
> Crandall, Texas
> Denton, Texas

44.The First State Bank in Ponder, Denton County, Texas (photo by author).

"Empty Bank Robbery"
Location: First State Bank, at the corner of FM 156 and West Bailey Street, Ponder, Texas.
Coordinates: 33.183173, -97.2895797
The Movie: Clyde, wanting to impress Bonnie, tries to rob the bank but finds out that it was bankrupt. Bonnie laughs at him.
The reality: Raymond Hamilton, not Clyde Barrow, attempted to rob a closed-down bank.

"Clyde wants to impress Bonnie"
Location: Walnut Street and Second Street, Venus, Texas.

Coordinates: 32.433136, -97.105712

The Movie: Clyde, who had just met Bonnie after trying to steal her mother's car and wants to impress her, robs Ritt's Groceries.

The reality: Clyde met Bonnie at a mutual friend's house. Their first robbery together occurred in Mabank, Texas; this attempt at criminality landed Bonnie in the Kaufman jail for several weeks.

45. The building that pretended to be Ritt's Groceries is now a church in downtown Venus (photo by author).

"Grocery Store Murder"

Location: Main Street and First Street, Maypearl, Texas.
Coordinates: 32.308798, -97.0144739

The movie: Clyde goes "grocery shopping" with a pistol. A clerk accosts him with a meat cleaver and Clyde shoots him dead. Clyde feels great remorse for this crime.

The reality: This scene is a recreation of the murder of Howard Hall at the S.R. Little Grocery Store at 624 S. Vaden in Sherman, Texas. The actual grocery store in Sherman no longer exists.

"Bank Robbery in Mineola"

Location: 102 Waller Street, Red Oak, Texas.
Coordinates: 32.5134991, -96.8070977

The movie: Bonnie and Clyde successfully hold up a bank in an incredibly busy downtown. After the robbery, the alarm bell rings and neither Bonnie nor Clyde can find their get-a-way car, which C.W. Moss had parked farther away than planned. In the ensuing escape, Clyde shoots a man who had jumped on his car's running board.

The reality: W.D. Jones maintained to the Dallas Police that he did not take part in any bank robberies. The gang never robbed a bank in Mineola and did not kill anyone as they robbed banks.

46. Although Red Oak is a burgeoning suburb of Dallas, its old downtown, used to stage a bank robbery scene in the movie, looks deserted (photo by author).

47. Pilot Point's former bank is an antique store in 2021 (photo by author).

"Bank robbery"
Location: Farmers and Merchants Bank, northwest corner of North Washington and West Main streets, Pilot Point, Texas.
Coordinates: 33.395785, -96.9606213
The movie: Bonnie and Clyde stage another successful bank robbery and make a clean get-away in this fast montage of their exploits.
The reality: The Farmer and Merchant's Bank in Pilot Point, Texas was never robbed by the gang; the film makers probably simply wanted a scenic bank in a town that looked thirty years older. Today, the town of Pilot Point celebrates the "Bonnie and Clyde Festival" where the pretend-robbery is reenacted.

"Downtown Arcadia on Death Day"
Location: 112-114 South Main Street, Crandall, Texas.
Coordinates: 32.6273665, -96.4558708
The movie: Bonnie and Clyde shop for sandwiches and other little items in downtown Arcadia, Louisiana. They are having a great time and enjoy each other's company. Bonnie buys a little trinket that brings her joy, then feeds an apple to a romantic Clyde. Tellingly, Bonnie wears a white, puffed sleeve dress, as to accentuate her unknowing innocence on that day, and Clyde wears a dapper suit vest with a white shirt. He loses a lens on his sunglasses, as if foreshadowing what is about to happen to his face.
The reality: Prior to their rendezvous with the ambush posse on the Mt. Lebanon Road, Bonnie and Clyde bought sandwiches and cigarettes at the Cranfield Café in Gibsland. Bonnie donned a red dress, red shoes, and a white and red hat. Around her neck is a crucifix, and on her chest is an acorn broach. She also sported a rather expensive wristwatch and still donned her wedding ring. She may have been reading one of the many true crime magazines she kept on the stolen car's floorboard. Clyde wore a blue shirt without a suit jacket and a pair of shades. The lens was most likely still intact as he wore them when he was gunned down; after all, he was driving southeast, against the sun, on the morning of May 23, 1934.

48. Denton's Campus Theater now holds live productions (photo by author).

Bonnie and Clyde World Premier
Location: Campus Theater, 214 W. Hickory Street, Denton, Texas.
Coordinates: 33.2148841, -97.1367382
What's to See: As you wind your way to Denton, you'll pass the lakeside city of Lake Dallas, where Clyde and his fellow gang-members hid out from the law (their camp site is under Lewisville Lake now). On West Hickory Street near downtown Denton sits the Campus Theater with its lovely neon sign. Today, community art councils and university students perform plays here, but in 1967 the theater hosted the premier of the movie, "Bonnie and Clyde."

Tour 3 — The Dallas-Fort Worth Road Trip

A tour of the places that surround the city of Dallas offers a glimpse into the lives of not only Bonnie and Clyde, but also of the regular people who lived in the area during the Great Depression. The cities and counties on this tour comprise the greater Dallas/Fort Worth Metroplex and follows the old road frequented by the Barrow Gang.

Unfortunately, many of the places where real, tangible history for the lives of Bonnie Parker and Clyde Barrow no longer exist. In the 1930s, the county jails in McLennan, and Kaufman counties (where Clyde and /or Bonnie spent time) tended to look like smaller versions of the county courthouses. Today, the outdated structures have been razed, and modern jails have taken their places. The homes where Bonnie Parker once lived have also been demolished. The houses rented by Emma Parker along Fish Trap Road, Cockrell Hill Road, Crockett Street, Douglas Avenue, Hickory Street, and Lamar Avenue have been replaced by warehouses, widened roads, condos, and in one instance, by the Winspear Opera House.

Many of the locations around Dallas where Clyde Barrow and his associates committed their crimes have also been lost to time. Clyde's first "official" foray into crime occurred in Denton, where he and his brother Buck tried to steal the safe from a gas station; the gas station is now a non-descript telecommunication structure. The "suburban grocery store" at 624 S. Vaden Street in Sherman where Clyde allegedly killed meat-cutter Howard Hall has been demolished, too. One of the most infamous robberies committed by the Barrow Gang was at the Neuhoff Packing Plant in August of 1932, in which the criminals stole the company's entire payroll. This location has now been swallowed by the Victory Park development, which centers on the American Airlines Center in downtown Dallas.

Interestingly, several of the banks that Raymond Hamilton held up still stand, and they are part of this tour. This tour brings the travelers to locations where the sites of crimes and contemporary activities can still be viewed and appreciated.

Robert H. Brock Hardware Store
Calaboose in Kemp
Bank in Lancaster
Cedar Hill Bank
Sowers Ambush
Top'o'the Hill Terrace
Fort Worth Stockyards
Grapevine Calaboose
Home Bank in Grapevine
Dove Road
First National Bank in Lewisville

49.Bonnie and Ralph Fults spent an uncomfortable night at the Kemp Calaboose (photo by author).

Robert H. Brock Hardware Store
Location: 109 E. Market Street, Mabank, Texas.
Coordinates: 32.3665025, -96.1025901
What's to See: The building that housed the hardware store that Clyde, Bonnie, and Ralph Fults attempted to rob in 1932 has been restored into a quaint gift shop/boutique.

Kemp Calaboose
Location: Alley behind southern side of Kemp's Main Street, Kemp, Kaufman County, Texas.
Coordinates: 32.4418298, -96.2306164
What's to See: After the botched hardware store robbery in Mabank, Clyde fled and left Bonnie and his friend, Ralph Fults, to their own devices. Bonnie and Ralph were caught and locked up in the town's lone jail, a brick structure

just in the back of the police station. After spending a very uncomfortable night, Bonnie was taken to the Kaufman County jail in Kaufman. Her mother refused to bail her out, hoping she'd come to her senses. Didn't work, did it?

50. Only the tile floor remains of the bank in Lancaster (photo by author).

Ruins of R.P. Henry Bank
Location: Corner of East Main and Henry streets, Lancaster, Texas.
Coordinates: 32.592079, -96.7557572
What's to See: The bank that Clyde and Raymond Hamilton robbed, located a block east off the downtown square, is now only a vacant lot, though the original flooring can still be seen. Once home to the town's heritage museum in its latter years, the bank's building became victim to a violent tornado in the 1990s. After this robbery, Clyde and Raymond split ways because Clyde believed Raymond had pocketed more than his fair share.

Sowers Road Ambush Site
Location: Vicinity of West Pioneer Drive and Irving Boulevard north of Grand Prairie and west of Irving, Texas.
Coordinates: 32.815699, -96.9622077
Coordinates: 32.746075,-96.9652247 (Hensley Field)
What's to See: In November of 1933, Dallas Sherriff Smoot Schmid and a posse failed an ambush on Bonnie and Clyde, who were meeting their family for a Thanksgiving reunion along the "Devil's Back Porch." This shooting occurred on Sowers Road "eight miles north of Grand Prairie," according to the Fort Worth Star Telegram. Sowers was once a farming community that has now been completely absorbed by Irving. Today, Sowers Road is West Pioneer Drive. In the 1930s, this road extended west from Eagle Ford Road

beyond the Trinity River, but today, Loop 12 cuts off the thoroughfare. The ambush site was on Sowers Road past Meyers Road, now MacArthur Road. After the shooting in which both Bonnie and Clyde were shot through the knees, their abandoned car was found "near the Hensley Flying Field" on the east side of Grand Prairie along U.S. 80/ Jefferson Boulevard. To reach Hensley Field, the couple drove south on Belt Line Road.[156]

51. The guardhouse at Top of the Hill Terrace, a former speak-easy (photo by author).

Top o' the Hill Terrace
Location: Arlington Baptist College, 3001 West Division Street, Arlington, Texas.
Coordinates: 32.7385836, -97.1577348,17.29
What's to See: U.S. 180 is the original road that connected Dallas to Fort Worth. Paved and improved in the 1920s, the road is also known as the Fort Worth Pike, Bankhead Highway, and "Old US 80." In downtown Arlington (Division Street), U.S. 80 intersected with the former Texas Military Road at what is now Center Street. Many of the buildings and houses encountered along this highway will be the same that Bonnie and Clyde saw as they drove this road so many years ago.

The quiet campus of the Arlington Baptist College was once much more active. During the late 1920s, this place was known as the "Top of the Hill Terrace," a gambling and sporting saloon near the Arlington Downs Racetrack where the hoi polloi as well as Dallas and Fort Worth's shady characters liked to hang out. It is not known if Bonnie and Clyde ever frequented this place, but because this was a speakeasy during Prohibition, they may have felt safe enough from the laws to grab a quick bite to eat and something to drink.

Many of the original sandstone structures left over from when the place was a speakeasy are used by the college. Under the campus bookstore is an escape tunnel, which patrons would use during raids. The tunnel's exit can be seen on the hill beneath the bookstore on the west side of the campus.

Fort Worth Stockyards Hotel

Location: Fort Worth Stockyards National Historic District, 109 East Exchange Avenue, Fort Worth, Texas.

Coordinates: 32.7890117, -97.3498017

What's to See: If driving the U.S. 80/ Bankhead Highway route into Fort Worth, the roads to the stockyards take the traveler through the heart of Fort Worth's historic underbelly: the area around the Convention Center used to be Fort Worth's notorious Hell's Half Acre. Up until the 1960s, bars, pawn shops, liquor stores, and topless venues turned profits here, and the grand hall for the city's chapter of the Ku Klux Klan, built in 1924, stands empty north of the courthouse at 1012 North Main Street.

52. The Fort Worth Stockyards have become an international tourist attraction (photo by author).

During the 1930s, the Stockyards were not as clean and friendly as they seem now. Large slaughterhouses churned out all sorts of meat products at the eastern end of the district, so millions of cattle, sheep, and pigs lined the pens. Cowboys, gamblers, outlaws, and businessmen partied, conducted trade, and slept here amid the noise and smells.

According to the hotel, Bonnie and Clyde spent a night in room 305 at the Stockyards Hotel at the corner of North Main Street and Exchange Avenue. Supposedly, a gun belonging to Bonnie was found inside one of the bedrooms. Despite the provenance displayed in the room, this is still an unsubstantiated claim — but far be it from me to dispute Bonnie and Clyde rumors!

53. The calaboose in Grapevine was moved to Main Street as a tourist attraction (photo by author).

Grapevine Calaboose
Location: Southwest corner of Franklin and Main streets in downtown Grapevine.
Coordinates: 32.9363399, -97.0790445
What's to See: The Grapevine Highway is a vintage road, but development has obliterated many of the older structures and landscapes. Grapevine itself, however, has become a very nice tourist center, with lots of shops and restaurants that try to maintain the historic village feel of the city.

The rounded calaboose housed Odell Chambless and Les Stewart on January 6, 1933 after their robbery of thee Home Bank just up the street. The calaboose was originally located behind the police station but was moved to become a tourist attraction along Main Street. This is the robbery that spurred the Tarrant County Sheriff's office to surveil the home of Lillian McBride in West Dallas the next day in the hope of finding their third suspect. Clyde Barrow shot Deputy Malcolm Davis instead.

Home Bank
Location: 404 S. Main Street, Grapevine.
Coordinates: 32.937531, -97.0789502

What's to See: The bank robbed by Odell Chambless and Les Stewart on January 6, 1933 led to their arrest and stay inside Grapevine's calaboose. The next day, Deputy Malcolm Davis, who was surveilling the "safe house" on County Line Avenue (now, Winnetka Avenue; see Tour 1) was **shot and killed** in a surprise encounter with Clyde Barrow. Today, the bank houses a local business.

Easter Sunday Murder Site
Location: Dove Road and TX 114, Grapevine.
Coordinates: 32.9698129, -97.1563295
What's to See: Dove was once a small, rural community close to the Tarrant County/Denton County line. Near the intersection of Dove Road and TX 114, Clyde and Henry Methvin killed two motorcycle troopers, Edward Bryan Wheeler and H.D. Murphy, on Easter Sunday, 1934. Due to rapid development, the area does not look like it did in the 1930s, though as of this writing, there are still patches of nature surrounding the site. Parking around the handsome granite marker memorializing the victims is difficult, so take caution.

First State Bank
Location: 515 Cedar Street, Cedar Hill.
Coordinates: 32.588826, -96.958436
What's to See: In October and again in November of 1932, Raymond Hamilton robbed this bank in broad daylight. The second robbery was committed with accomplice Les Stewart. The little building still stands as a private business.

First National Bank of Lewisville
Location: 165 West Main Street, Lewisville.
Coordinates: 33.0465724, -96.9979663
What's to See: In 1934, Raymond Hamilton committed his last crime when he robbed the First National Bank of Lewisville, which was located on the bottom floor of a two-story building on the north side of downtown at the intersection of Main and Poydras Streets. When Raymond left the scene, he did so by following US 77 (Mill Street) north. If you drive north on Mill Street today, you'll end up in Lake Lewisville; the old highway was drowned when Lake Dallas was expanded in 1948. At the intersection of Main and Kealy Streets is a restaurant, which is located in what used to be the town doctor's residence. The doctor supposedly was kidnapped, blindfolded, and brought to the Barrow Gang's hideout at Lake Dallas to treat their wounds.

54. The First National Bank only occupied half of the bottom floor in downtown Lewisville. A telephone exchange and the city's newspaper occupied the remainder of the building when Raymond Hamilton robbed the bank in 1934 (photo by author).

Tour 4 — The Louisiana Road Trip

Bonnie and Clyde did not frequent Louisiana much during their short lifetimes. They tended to stay around Dallas so that they could visit their families and drove north to hide commit crimes. While they were very familiar with East Texas towns like Texarkana, Waskom, and Longview, where they sometimes stayed with Cumie Barrow's relatives, they did not rob banks or payrolls further east. The only recorded crime they committed in Louisiana was kidnapping a man and woman after stealing the owner's car in Ruston.

It was upon Henry Methvin's suggestion that the couple made their way to Louisiana after the murder of Constable Cal Campbell near Miami, Oklahoma. The Methvins were an old family in northwestern Louisiana and knew the lay of the land intimately. According to early reports, Clyde Barrow had bought a farm near Alabama Bend to act as a hideout under Ivy Methvin, Henry's father, name. However, this farm was surveilled.[157] Thus, Henry found an abandoned cabin near Sailes at Black Lake Bayou where the couple could stay hidden from locals and the authorities. The actual location of this hide-out is still speculated. The Shreveport Journal described it as "vacant house in an isolated section of the parish, two miles from Sailes."[158]

It was hard for Bonnie and Clyde to stay hidden in this sparsely populated slice of Louisiana; not only were they newcomers with Clyde claiming to be a chairmaker, but they also drove a "new, sandy-colored Ford V-8" with Arkansas plates.[159] They frequently left their hideout to take trips to Arcadia, Bentonville, and Shreveport. The terrain was heavily wooded and hilly, making visibility difficult. And, unlike the more familiar North Texas region, this new area did not have many alternate routes. In order for them to return to their hideout, they only had the option of driving on one or two paved roads — the many logging paths that crossed the area usually went nowhere.

This tour brings the traveler along U.S. 80, the federal highway that connected Dallas to Shreveport. A few vintage Depression-era sites can still be appreciated along this road.

U.S. 80
St. Paul's Bottom
Site of Majestic Cafe, Shreveport
Ma Canfield's Café, Gibsland
Ambush Site, between Mt. Lebanon and Sailes
Conger Furniture Store, Arcadia

55. In Shreveport, U.S. 80 becomes Texas Street closer to downtown. This used to be the busiest strip in town, but upon building Interstate 20, most of the businesses shuttered (photo by author).

U.S. 80

Old federal highway that links Georgia to California
Dallas, Texas to Shreveport, Louisiana (190 miles)
What's to See: At the turn of the 20th century, the road that would become U.S. 80 was labeled the "Dixie Overland Trail" by automobile tourists. After road improvements became state and federal concerns, this highway received its numerical designation in 1926. Bonnie and Clyde traveled this road often, as they sometimes spent the night at the home of Cumie Barrow's relatives in East Texas. Now bypassed by Interstate 20, the older highway passes through the downtown areas of several towns, such as Mineola and Marshall. Jefferson, the seat of Marion County about twenty miles north of Marshall

on U.S. 59, is worth a stop for its architecture and history as an inland deep water port in the 19th century.

Around Waskom, a Texas town on U.S. 80 just west of the Louisiana border, Joe Palmer, a one-time gang member who was sprung out of jail during the Eastham Prison Raid, killed Wade McNabb, a former fellow prison inmate, whom he believed to be a police informant. Joe Palmer was later executed in Huntsville on the same day as Raymond Hamilton.

Once in Louisiana, U.S. 80 travels through the old town of Greenwood before entering Shreveport. In Shreveport, U.S. 80 is Texas Street. Several old motor courts and abandoned businesses line the once-busy thoroughfare. Texas Street brings the traveler into downtown.

56. Dilapidated shotgun houses, a simple architectural style that was found in cities throughout the American South in the 20th century, line some streets near St. Paul's Bottom in Shreveport (photo by author).

St. Paul's Bottom
Location: A razed neighborhood that historically was bounded by Christian, Common, Fannin Streets and Cross Bayou, west of downtown Shreveport. The Bottom can be reached via Texas Street (U.S. 80).
Coordinates: 32.514571, -93.7552397

What's to see: Today, nothing remains of the storied entertainment district that fed the talents of legendary musicians like Huddie "Lead Belly" Ledbetter. Originally a freedman's town that centered around St. Paul's Methodist Church, the city zoned this area to be a legal vice district at the turn of the 20th century.[160] The area was decommissioned as a vice zone in 1917, but the clubs, parlors, and brothels remained, eventually extending closer to Texas Street. During the brief time that Bonnie Parker and Clyde Barrow "resided" in northwestern Louisiana, some of the establishments and mansions located on higher ground from the vice district had become parlors, saloons, and brothels.

Like the entry for Top o' the Hill Terrace in Arlington (see Tour 2), the inclusion of St. Paul's Bottom on his tour is based on conjecture: the couple may have frequented the location for access to alcohol and gambling games (though at this point, they may have been "too hot" to appear anywhere for long). However, even without actual Bonnie and Clyde provenance, recognizing the history of St. Paul's Bottom is key to identifying some of the places along Texas Street, the original main road that connected Dallas to Shreveport. For example, the musical enticements from St. Paul's Bottom carried over to the nearby Shreveport Municipal Auditorium at Texas Street and Grand Avenue, where the famous "Louisiana Hayride" broadcasted from 1948 to 1960.

57. What was once the Majestic Café in Shreveport (photo by author).

Majestic Café (defunct)
Location: 422 Milam Street, Shreveport.
Coordinates: 32.5122665, -93.7508235
What's to See: Shreveport lies directly on the Red River. A former Caddo village, it grew into a city due to the clearing of a large log jam by Captain Henry Shreve in the 1830s, which allowed the Red River to be navigable above Natchitoches. Steam-driven paddlewheel boats made Shreveport into a major shipping port, and several rail roads came through the town after the Civil War.

Today, with its glittering casinos, brick warehouses, and wrought-iron architecture, downtown Shreveport is a mix of old and new. The town experienced a building boom in the 1920s, so Art-Deco buildings abound. The former location of the Majestic Café occupies the ground floor of one of these buildings. A few days before the ambush, Henry Methvin ordered sandwiches for Bonnie, Clyde and himself here. While he waited on the order inside the restaurant, Bonnie and Clyde, who were sitting in the car, raced away upon spotting a police cruiser. Clyde's erratic driving roused suspicion, and the officers briefly chased the couple. When the police told the Texas Ambush Posse about their encounter, the stage was set for the ambush. However, Henry Methvin may have separated himself from Bonnie and Clyde on purpose to aid in the ambush.

Canfield's Café (now a museum)
Location: 2419 Main Street, Gibsland.
Coordinates: 32.5447591, -93.0554658
What's to See: Bonnie and Clyde bought their last meal from Canfield's Café in Gibsland; a sandwich was found half-eaten on Bonnie's lap after the ambush. Today, the old café is the "Bonnie and Clyde Ambush Museum," an informative museum dedicated to the crime duo. The museum displays photos, guns, the 1967 movie car, and houses a research archive. Other businesses along Main Street provide information about the ambush as well. Every year around May 23, the town of Gibsland hosts the Bonnie and Clyde Festival, complete with reenactments.

Ambush Site
Location: LA 154 South between Mt. Lebanon and Sailes, Bienville Parish.
Coordinates: 32.443002, -93.0942867
What's to See: Upon leaving Gibsland on LA 154, note a dark, red brick building to your left. This is the former elementary school, where kids streamed out on the day of the ambush to gawk at the dead outlaws. On the way to the ambush marker, take a look at the antebellum dogtrot houses (dogtrots are houses with an open breezeway through the middle) in and around Mount Lebanon, a cute little village nestled in the Louisiana pine. Bonnie and Clyde's last hideout, further south near Sailes, was also described as a dogtrot cabin (this cabin no longer exists).

The ambush road does not look like it did when Bonnie and Clyde drove to their doom. LA 154 has been paved, has become wider, and the trees that once surrounded it have been trimmed away from the edges of the road. As you crest a small hill and make your way towards the ambush

58. A marker along LA 154 commemorates the ambush of Bonnie and Clyde. This photo, taken in 2008, reflects the marker's current state: it is consistently vandalized and repaired (photo by author).

BARROW AND PARKER WOMAN SHOT DEAD NEAR GIBSLAND

59. Headline in the Shreveport Times, whose correspondent was the first to report on the ambush (May 23, 1934)).

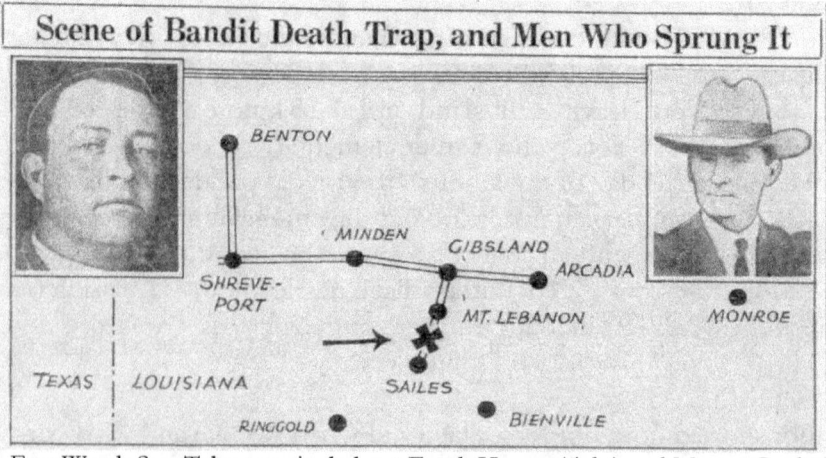

60. The Fort Worth Star Telegram singled out Frank Hamer (right) and Manny Gault (left) as the masterminds of the ambush (May 24, 1934).

marker, you will need to use your imagination to picture what the highway looked like all those years ago.

Think about the ambush posse, consisting of Frank Hamer, Manny Gault, Bob Alcorn, Ted Hinton, Prentiss Oakley, and Henderson Jordan, hiding in the thickets, slapping at mosquitoes, and smelling of cigarettes and stale coffee. Imagine Ivy Methvin's pick-up truck parked in the middle of the road, leaning crookedly on a jack. Listen for the sound of a new, very powerful Ford barreling down the road as if the driver was late to his appointment with hell.

The site where Bonnie and Clyde met their ends is commemorated by a large concrete slab that was erected by Bienville Parish. The marker has been repaired several times as it is often pocked by bullet holes and spray painted with graffiti. A number of small camp sites, with trash strewn about, surround the immediate vicinity.

In 2008 (and 2021), the marker text reads:

> "On this site May 23, 1934
> Clyde Barrow
> And
> Bonnie Parker
> Were killed by
> Law Enforcement Officials"

Conger Furniture Store and Funeral Parlor

Location: Railroad Street, Arcadia.
Coordinates: 32.548637, -92.9218027
What's to See: After the ambush, the bullet-riddled car (with Bonnie and Clyde still inside) was towed to the parish seat, Arcadia. The bodies were laid out to be examined by the coroner at Conger's Furniture Store. In this period, small town furniture stores doubled as morgues due to their ability to store and move caskets. Conger's does not exist anymore — the building, damaged by wind and weather, is long gone. In 2008, its floor was still visible. In 2021, a park now occupies the downtown space.

Across from Conger's Furniture Store and Funeral Parlor is the wooden Bienville Depot, which has been turned into a museum that displays photos of the infamous day when Arcadia became a town known around the world.

Downtown Arcadia has antique stores and restaurants to make your trip complete. Every month, Arcadia hosts Bonnie and Clyde Trade Days. These "trade days," which take place on the third weekend of each month, consist of a giant flea market and sometimes, reenactments.

61. Not much was left of the Conger Furniture Store in downtown Arcadia, Louisiana, in 2008. In 2021, this empty shell had been converted to a pocket park (photo by author).

Tour 5 — The North of Texas Road Trip

One fascinating aspect in the story of Bonnie and Clyde is Barrow's reliance on automobiles. Unlike any other gangster from the era, Clyde made his car into a defensive weapon as well as his home. After the killing of Malcolm Davis in 1932, he and Bonnie were never able to live in West Dallas again. While they attempted to find respite in places like Joplin, Fort Smith, and Platte City, they learned quickly that they had become prey for law enforcement. Clyde drove continuously and constantly, with Bonnie by his side, covering hundreds of miles along muddy backroads in a single day. Their deaths inside yet another stolen automobile, a brand new Ford V-8, were a fitting end to gangsters who took advantage of the era's modern technologies.

Due to their notoriety in Texas, the Barrow Gang committed most of their crimes far from Dallas, especially their bank robberies. According to police reports and FBI files, they held up banks in Lawrence, Kansas; Lucerne, Indiana; Rembrandt and Stuart, Iowa; Poteau, Oklahoma; and Van Buren, Arkansas. Interestingly, Bonnie did not participate in the actual robberies. Throughout most of 1933, she was at home in Dallas while Clyde ran with his fellow gang members. Afterwards, she accompanied Clyde consistently, but tended to remain in the car as the lookout or stayed behind at roadside motels during robberies. However, while W.D. Jones and her cousin Bess claimed she did not shoot guns, this was probably not true. She apparently fired during several shoot-outs.

This tour travels through Oklahoma, Arkansas, Kansas, Missouri, and Iowa to places that the Barrow Gang robbed and frequented. Violence was a constant companion in this period of their short lives: most of their murders, and violence perpetrated against them, were committed north of their home state. The sites are listed in chronological order.

- Lawrence, Kansas
- Stringtown, Oklahoma
- Oronogo, Missouri
- Joplin, Missouri
- Alma, Arkansas
- Dexter, Iowa
- Perry, Iowa
- Rembrandt, Iowa
- Poteau, Oklahoma
- Commerce, Oklahoma

Stuart, Iowa

First National Bank, alleged bank robbery in January of 1932
Location; 746 Massachusetts Street, Lawrence, Kansas.
Coordinates: 38.9695414, -95.2362133
What's to see: According to Ralph Fults, Clyde Barrow and Raymond Hamilton got their start at robbing banks at the First National Bank in Lawrence, Kansas, where they absconded with about $33,000. No newspaper accounts, police reports, or eyewitnesses corroborate this account, however.

Site of "Dance Hall Shooting" in August of 1932
Location: Southbound side of U.S. 69 (Mississippi Avenue) between Ash Street and Lake Shore Drive, Stringtown, Oklahoma.
Coordinates: 34.462923, -96.0634327
What's to See: Stringtown is not the most cosmopolitan place now, and it wasn't back when Clyde, Raymond Hamilton, and Everett Mulligan decided to attend a country dance here in 1932. When two officers approached them, the gangsters shot them, killing Deputy Sheriff Eugene Moore. Today, the murder is commemorated by a state historical marker.

62. Oronogo is a mining town that no longer sees mining. Its bank was Bonnie Parker's first robbery (photo by author).

Farmers & Miners Bank, site of robbery December of 1932
Location: West Main and First Streets, Oronogo, Missouri.
Coordinates: 37.188112, -94.4705252
What to See: After Thanksgiving in 1932, Clyde, Bonnie, and two early members of the first iteration of the "Lake Dallas Gang," Frank Hardy and Hollis Hale, robbed the Farmers & Miners Bank in this once-busy town and netted about $500. The cashier shot at the two men inside the bank, who returned fire with sub-machine guns. After the robbery, the men jumped into a Chevrolet idling "in front of the bank where the driver was doing a good deal of tooting." They then exchanged this car for a Ford V-8 "driven by a woman:" Bonnie Parker, in her first-ever bank robbery.[161]

Not much remains of Oronogo's downtown, as the mines that brought wealth are no longer functioning. Surrounding the town are large piles of slag from the mines, and contamination of the soil and water has led the Environmental Protection Agency to designate the old mine a superfund site. The robbed bank partially stands at the corner of West Main and First Streets.

Joplin Garage Apartment, gang hideout in April of 1933
Location: 3347 ½ Oak Ridge Drive, Joplin, Missouri.
Coordinates: 37.0516877, -94.5191828
What's to See: Joplin is a large, busy city that has lead, zinc, and galena mining to thank for its existence. Clyde felt comfortable enough in Joplin to hide out for a while inside a garage apartment that had easy access for a quick get-a-way. Clyde, Bonnie, W.D. Jones, Buck Barrow, and Blanche Barrow rented this two bedroom flat in a middle-class neighborhood for about two weeks until their suspicious ways caught "the laws'" attention. While serving a search warrant, the gang fired on the officers, killing Harry McGinnis and Wes Harryman.

The garage apartment, built of native stone with wooden framing, still stands in this hilly section of Joplin. While the interiors have been redone and the neighborhood has become quite gentrified, the scene is relatively unchanged from what occurred so many years ago. Over the years, owners have changed the function of the apartment, sometimes making it into a bed and breakfast or a museum. Thankfully, the building, now listed on the National Register of Historic Places, was spared destruction from the F5 tornado that ravaged Joplin in 2011.

63. The Barrow gang's "Joplin Hideout" was a garage apartment in one of the prettiest neighborhoods in Joplin. Two law enforcement officers were murdered by the gang in this driveway (photo by author).

Joplin Mining Museum, artifacts from shooting at Joplin hideout, April of 1933

Location: 504 South Schifferdecker Avenue, Joplin, Missouri.
Coordinates: 37.0876824, -94.5528084
What's to see: The Joplin Mining Museum Complex at Schifferdecker Park is a large institution with many exhibits and warrants a lengthy visit. The Bonnie and Clyde connoisseur, however, should make a bee-line towards the back of the museum, where a display shows artifacts recovered from the Joplin Hideout. The original front door is mounted to the floor, though make sure to note that the holes in the door are not due to the famous shoot-out but are the result of a domestic disturbance that occurred years later. Also on display are two necklaces found among the many items in the apartment. That the museum even owns these artifacts is surprising in itself. Law enforcement officers, journalists, and curiosity seekers often took whatever they wanted during the confusion following the shoot-outs, and most of these items remain in the hands of their descendants and/or collectors to this day.

Commercial Bank, alleged bank robbery in June of 1933

Location: 614 Fayetteville Road, Alma, Arkansas.
Coordinates: 35.4785134, -94.2237007
Coordinates: 35.423688, -94.3770197 (former Midway Motor Court in Fort Smith, Arkansas)
What's to See: After Clyde, Bonnie, and W.D. Jones plunged into the Red River near Wellington, Texas, the criminals eventually made their way to Fort Smith, Arkansas after meeting up with Buck and Blanche Barrow. Here, they stayed inside a cabin at the Twin Cities Motor Court, formerly known as the Midway Motor Court at the northeast corner of Midland Boulevard (U.S. 64) and 50th Street (once, Waldron Road) where Clyde tended to Bonnie's wounds.[162] According to accounts, Clyde explained that Bonnie had suffered a burn during a campfire cookout. Clyde raced to Dallas to ask Billie, Bonnie's sister, to return with him and nurse Bonnie.

64. Today, no trace exists of the Twin Cities Tourist Court in Fort Smith nor Brown Grocery Store in Van Buren, but the bank building in Alma, which most likely was not robbed by the Barrow Gang, still stands (photo by author).

In the meantime, Buck and W.D. Jones may have robbed the Commercial Bank in nearby Alma, Arkansas and in the process, tied up Constable Hubert Humphries. There is doubt about this robbery, however. The bank robbery netted the thieves over $3,000 but, according to their families, the Barrow Gang was desperate for money at this time. They were so desperate, in fact, that Buck Barrow and W.D. Jones held up the Brown Grocery Store at 111 West Lafayette Street in Fayetteville instead.[163] As all law enforcement officers were on high alert after the bank robbery, anyway, the Barrow Gang did not get far in their getaway. Marshal Humphries spotted them, gave chase, and Buck Barrow shot him with a machine gun during a brief gun battle.[164]

65. A neon sign greets the visitor to Dexter, Iowa (photo by author).

Dexfield Park, site of ambush in July of 1933
Location: Dexfield Road (P 48) approximately eight miles north of Dexter, Iowa and eight miles south of Redfield, Iowa.
Coordinates: 41.563833, -94.2324867
Coordinates: 39.3111151,-94.6827542 (Red Crown Tourist Court, Platte City, Missouri)
What's To See: A roadside historical marker at Raccoon River.
Dexter lies on the "White Pole Road," which was built in 1910 as a state-of-the-art highway linking Des Moines to Council Bluffs, and this road made Dexfield Park a tourist destination. The park, which opened in 1915, boasted a cement swimming pool, diving board, picnic grounds, petting zoo, hiking trails, and canoe rentals. By 1933, the park had been closed for several years.

After their short stay in Fort Smith, Clyde, Bonnie, Buck, Blanche, and W.D. Jones decided to hide at the Red Crown Tourist Court just south of Platte City, Missouri to continue nursing Bonnie. A devastating gun battle between the Barrow Gang and local police ensued. Blanche sustained eye injuries from flying glass and Buck was shot in the head.

The Red Crown Tourist Court and Tavern was built to look like castles and remained popular hang-outs in Platte City well into the 1960s. A fire destroyed the buildings and today, no trace of them remains. The buildings were located at the junctions of U.S. 71 and U.S. 59, which is now an empty field across from the Kansas City International Airport, and the site is commemorated by a state historical marker. A decade or so ago, some enterprising souls managed to salvage bricks from the court and sell them to tourists, so bits and pieces of the Red Crown are still floating around.

The Barrow Gang, badly wounded after the shootout at the Red Court Tourist Camp in Platte City, decided to hide out in the woods near the Raccoon River. The abandoned amusement park between Dexter and Redfield offered the gang plenty advantages: the fields were still relatively clear, but the underbrush offered good cover; small trails made a quick get-a-way easier; and the location by the river provided a good water source.

An ambush posse was formed after Clyde's presence in town aroused suspicion. The party surprised the gang in the early morning of July 24, 1933. Clyde, Bonnie, and W.D. Jones were able to shoot their way out. Buck, who had sustained a head wound during the Platte City shoot-out, and Blanche, whose eyes had been hurt by flying glass when the car's window was struck, were left behind. Blanche surrendered and was taken into custody. Buck was brought to the King's Daughters Hospital in Perry, where he died a few days later.

Today, Dexfield Park is remembered only by a granite marker on the west side of the Raccoon River. Plowed fields have replaced the swimming pool, and a private farm stands now on the site where the shoot-out took place. Bonnie, Clyde, and W.D. crossed the Raccoon River to escape the posse. While resting along the Raccoon River under the brush, Bonnie had asked W.D. to shoot her if Clyde didn't return after he had set off to steal another automobile.

Some Bonnie and Clyde researchers maintain that Dexfield Park proved to be the gang's Waterloo. The gun fight was definitely a turning point, as Buck died, Blanche was sent to prison, and W.D. Jones deserted the gang. Clyde had to find new gang members to continue his path of destruction, which led to the Eastham Raid and ultimately, his own demise.

King's Daughters Hospital, site of Buck Barrow's death in July of 1933
Location: 2323 Willis Avenue, Perry, Iowa.
Coordinates: 41.8382314, -94.0921399
What's to see: After the ambush at Dexfield Park, Blanche Barrow was taken into custody. She was jailed at Platte City, Missouri (the city's jail is no longer standing) and she never saw her husband again. Buck was brought to the King's Daughters Hospital in Perry, where he was treated for his head and body wounds. As he faced death, his mother Cumie traveled to Perry to be with her son, who called out for her multiple times (though he may have also called for Blanche; husbands and wives from the era sometimes referred to their spouses as "momma/mother" and "daddy"). Buck didn't succumb to bullet wounds, though; he died of pneumonia on July 29, 1933. Before his demise, he was visited by officials from Alma, Arkansas, where he confessed to having shot Marshal Henry Humphries.

The building where Buck died was replaced by a newer facility in the 1960s, but still functions as a health care facility.

First National Bank, site of robbery in January of 1934
Location: West Main Street, Rembrandt, Iowa.
Coordinates: 42.8255148, -95.1711948
What's to see: After the Eastham Prison Raid, the newly-formed Barrow Gang sought to net as much money as they could from bank hold-ups. In Rembrandt, a tiny town in the middle of Iowa cornfields, "four bandits held up the First National bank and fled with between $3,000 and $4,000 in cash." Two of the robbers went inside the bank, both described as young and light-complected. The other two were inside the waiting get-a-way car, a Ford sedan. Bonnie was not at the scene. She apparently was hiding out with another vehicle that they swapped out after the bank robbery.

The old bank building is no longer in use but can be seen along the north side of Main Street.

Central National Bank, site of robbery in January of 1934
Location: Southwest corner of Dewey Avenue and South McKenna Street, Poteau, Oklahoma.
Coordinates: 35.0515187, -94.6242746
What's to see: After the robbery in Rembrandt, Iowa, Clyde, Raymond Hamilton, Joe Palmer, and Henry Methvin robbed the Central National Bank in the pin-neat town of Poteau. Described as "well dressed" men in their thirties, they made the customers and bankers get on the floor and even

disarmed one of them without bloodshed. The getaway car, a dark Plymouth sedan, waited for them at the front of the bank. Like before, Bonnie remained at an undisclosed location, waiting for their return with the $1,200 they stole.[165]

The bank is no longer at this location, and the building has been substantially altered. Remains of the original building with its architectural oddities can be seen in the back alley.

66. The bank in Poteau, robbed by Clyde Barrow, Bonnie Parker, Raymond Hamilton, and Henry Methvin, was the second crime committed by the outlaws after the Eastham Prison Raid of January 1934 (photo by author)

Site of "Commerce Shooting" in April of 1934

Location: U.S. 69 (old Route 66), Miami and Commerce, Oklahoma.
Coordinates: 36.910587, -94.8797207 (Grand Army of the Republic Cemetery, where Constable Campbell is buried).
What's to see: Miami is a vibrant town that boasts one of the longest Route 66 Main Streets. Along Main Street, watch for the fabulous Coleman's Theater, a stunning vaudeville showplace in the Art Deco style, and several cafes, museums, and stores catering to the Route 66 traveler. Main Street is now U.S. 69.

Follow U.S. 69 north into Commerce, another vintage Route 66 town. Between the two towns are the Lost Trail and Crab Apple mines. It was near these mines where Clyde, Bonnie, and Henry Methvin parked along a dirt side road to take turns sleeping. As City Marshal Percy Boyd and Constable Cal Campbell came to investigate, Clyde shot Percy Boyd and took him hostage, while Henry Methvin shot and killed Cal Campbell. This proved to be the gang's last murder before their own demise a few weeks later in Louisiana.

67. An original stretch of old Route 66 south of Miami (photo by author).

Route 66

Coordinates: 36.8161, -94.9291277

Before you get to Miami, take a trip through time on an original stretch of Route 66. On U.S. 69 north of Narcissa and south of Miami, turn east (right) onto E140: you will find yourself on a narrow, concrete "ribbon road" of the now-decommissioned U.S. 66. A drive down this road will transport you back to the days of the Model T. Past many curves and dusty stretches (take extra precaution if it's raining), the road will lead to the fairgrounds in Miami. This original alignment meets up with Miami's Main Street north of the fairgrounds.

68. Unlike during the bank robbery in Poteau a few months prior, the Barrow Gang were disheveled and disorganized when robbing the First National Bank in Stuart, Iowa about a month before Bonnie and Clyde's deaths (photo by author).

First National Bank, site of robbery in April of 1934
Location: 100 NW 2nd Street, Stuart, Iowa.
Coordinates: 41.504732, -94.3190642
What's to see: Eight days after the murder of Constable Campbell, Bonnie waited in a dark Pontiac as "two unkempt bandits robbed the First National Bank" in downtown Stuart. The two "plainly nervous" men were Clyde Barrow and Henry Methvin. Before absconding with nearly $2,000, they forced the tellers and customers onto the floor of one of the bank's vaults, then locked them inside. The whole robbery took about five minutes, according to the newspaper account.[166]

The bank still stands at the corner of NW 2nd Street and North Division Street. A prominent sign tells the story of the robbery committed by Bonnie and Clyde.

Tour 6 — The Texas Road Trip

As Texas was their home state, Bonnie and Clyde continued to return there. Unfortunately, most of the places that has ties to Bonnie and Clyde are no longer extant, the sites are on private property, or their locations are nebulous. Waco is a perfect example. The McClellan County jail that once held Clyde, and from which Bonnie helped him escaped, has been replaced by a newer facility. Bonnie stayed at her newly-wed cousin's house in Waco so that she could visit him every day, but the address has been lost to time. The address of the house that Bonnie ransacked while looking for the gun is known, but the house itself no longer exists.

The Texas Road Trip, therefore, focuses on places that can still be visited.

    Huntsville, Texas
    Lovelady, Texas
    Waco, Texas
    Wellington, Texas

69. A pistol, taken from Bonnie after her death, is displayed at the Texas Prison Museum (photo by author).

Texas Prison Museum

Directions: 491 TX-75 North, Huntsville, Texas.

Coordinates: 30.7357157, -95.5866981

What's to See: The Texas Prison Museum displays a gun taken from Bonnie's corpse after the ambush. Informative posters tell about the 1934 Eastham Prison Raid. The wooden electric chair, nicknamed "Old Sparky," sits behind a three-walled partition. Used between 1924 and 1964, over 361 were killed in this chair, including Barrow associates Raymond Hamilton and Joe Palmer.

Raymond Hamilton had been sentenced to death for the murder of John Bucher and was considered a habitual criminal. After his capture in April 1935, he was rushed to the electric chair within a month. His girlfriend, Katie, and his mother sought to spare his destiny, but it was too late — still, until the hour of his death, Raymond hoped for a reprieve. None was forthcoming. While Joe Palmer had recognized his follies before his execution just a few hours prior, Raymond did not do this. He insisted that he had never killed a single man. When he entered the death chamber, he simply threw himself into the electric chair, resigned to his fate, and said, "Goodbye, all." His death by jolts of electricity took eight minutes.

70. Captain Joe Bird Cemetery is populated by dead prisoners, some of whom were executed. Raymond Hamilton's family claimed his body and buried him in a quiet memorial park in Dallas (photo by author).

Walls Unit
Location: 815 12th Street, Huntsville, Texas.
Coordinates: 30.722968, -95.546561
What's to See: The Walls (or Huntsville) Unit is the oldest state prison in Texas. Dominating downtown Huntsville like a medieval fortress, the imposing, red bricked Walls Unit was home to death row from 1928 to 1965[167] and also served the general prison population. The inmate infirmary was located here, too.

Buck Barrow served his penance at the Walls Unit, and Clyde recuperated here after having his toes chopped off to get out of the Eastham Prison Farm. Clyde also made wooden jewelry boxes inside the Walls Unit, one of which he gave to his sister-in-law, Blanche Barrow. After being sentenced to death for the murders of John Bucher and Major Crowson, respectively, Raymond Hamilton and Joe Palmer were executed in this prison in May of 1935.

Captain Joe Bird Cemetery
Location: 380 Bowers Boulevard, Huntsville, Texas.
Coordinates: 30.7127245, -95.540136
What's to see: Since the mid-nineteenth century, Captain Joe Byrd Cemetery has offered eternal rest for prisoners who died while in state custody and whose bodies were never collected by their next of kin. Chief Satanta of the Kiowas, who was charged with murder after a raid on the Warren Wagon Train near Fort Richardson in 1871 and committed suicide in prison, was once buried here, but his body was moved to the Fort Sill Cemetery for a more dignified burial. His old tombstone rests against a tree.

The stark white crosses in orderly rows only identify the dead by their prison numbers. Any grave marked with a discreet "X" means that the deceased was executed. While no Barrow associates are buried here, the cemetery is a fascinating reminder of the grisly world of crime and punishment.

Eastham State Prison Farm
Location: FM 230 south of Lovelady, Texas.
Coordinates: 30.977633, -95.630198
What's to see: For historians of Clyde Barrow, the Eastham State Prison Farm is a historic place indeed. Here, Clyde Barrow supposedly committed his first murder. Here, he turned into a "rattlesnake" under the back breaking labor and harsh treatment. Here, he had a fellow inmate cut off two toes in order to escape the work details. And here, Clyde staged a prison raid

that freed several inmates, including Raymond Hamilton and Henry Methvin, which ultimately led to his own demise.

The Eastham Unit sits less than a mile east of the Trinity River and is very isolated. Because Eastham Prison Farm is still an active jail, visitors need special permission to enter the site. The actual barrack of the prison farm where Clyde slept is now just a shell, but still stands.

Texas Ranger Museum
Location: 100 Texas Ranger Trail, Waco, Texas
Coordinates: 31.5560113, -97.1205115
What's to see: The Texas Ranger Museum celebrates the heritage of Texas' oldest law enforcement organization (and at times, controversial agency) with exhibits, archives, and a bookstore. The Barrow Gang Ambush permanent exhibit displays items taken from the bodies of Bonnie and Clyde (such as a pocket watch), weapons and license plates discovered in the "death car," and documents supporting the ambush, including expense account reports.

Weeks after the ambush, Clyde and Bonnie's parents wrote to the Rangers, requesting that the items taken from the car be returned to them. That plea fell on deaf ears — the only items the family ever received were the clothes that the couple wore when they were killed.

Salt Fork of the Red River, site of the accident in 1933
Location: US 83 north of Wellington, Texas.
Coordinates: 34.956175, -100.2224577
What's to see: Today, the Salt Fork of the Red River is bridged by utilitarian, concrete spans. Prior, two iron truss bridges have occupied this location. When Clyde, Bonnie, and W.D. Jones came to this section of Texas in 1933, the first iron truss bridge was set to be replaced by the second bridge and therefore, the road at this point was closed. Driving at his usual high rate of speed, Clyde ignored the warning signs that the bridge had been washed out and ended up plunging into the river bottom. The Pritchards, whose farm was located on a bluff close by, witnessed the accident and helped the bandits, especially Bonnie, whose severe burn on her leg left her with a limp for the rest of her short life.

Across the river is a quiet camp site where cement bridge pillars still stand. Those pillars are old pilings of the first bridge.

Note that the historical marker on US 83 commemorating the "plunge" is a little inaccurate. It mentions that Buck Barrow was with Bonnie and Clyde that night, but actually the third member was W.D. Jones.

71. Collingworth County's second iron truss bridge was erected in the mid-1930s, after Clyde's crash. This bridge was demolished in 2010 (photo by author).

Collingsworth County Museum
Location: 824 East Avenue, Wellington, Texas.
Coordinates: 34.8554781, -100.2151259
What's to see: The Collingsworth County Museum in downtown Wellington (824 East Avenue on the square in downtown Wellington) has pictures, newspaper articles, and artifacts pertaining to the Red River Plunge.

Tour 7 — Random Bonnie and Clyde

Romanticized and mythologized, Bonnie and Clyde appear in many places, often as figments of imagination. Like Bonnie wrote in her poem, The Story of Bonnie and Clyde, random robberies were often pinned on the gang in newspaper articles, and the general public often exaggerated of fantasized about interactions that most likely did not happen.

The "random" places in this tour are just that: random. These are places with bona-fide associations to Bonnie and Clyde's known history. Some places merit an actual, dedicated trip, while others are sites that can be encountered whenever (or if ever) the opportunity to visit presents itself.

Arbuckle Mountains
Location: U.S. 77 between Springer and Davis, Oklahoma.
Coordinates: 34.4253657, -97.1573841
What's to see: As US 77 winds around the Arbuckle Mountains between Springer and Davis, the vista becomes increasingly breathtaking. A scenic overlook at the top of a mountain offers a beautiful view of the valley where Turner Falls empties into Honey Creek. The waterfall, which at 70 feet is the tallest in Oklahoma, can be visited at the bottom of US 77 inside a park owned by the city of Davis. Two deep and clear swimming holes, the ruins of a castle, tourist cabins, souvenir shops, artists in residence, and even tipi lodges give the visitor the experience of being in a kind of time warp, when vacations were family-oriented, kitschy, and didn't have to involve major travel to be fun.

Along the road toward Davis, many other remnants of the Arbuckle Mountain's tourist days are still visible, including long abandoned tourist courts, cabin ruins, metal outlines of old neon signs, and even a defunct amusement park. Bonnie and Clyde hid out in these mountains and stayed in at least one of the tourist camps along this road, though which one is unknown. They would have felt right at home here because this stretch of highway was built by prison labor in the late 1920s.

Home of Elsie Stamps, Bonnie's aunt
Location: 522 N. Sixth Street, Carlsbad, New Mexico.
Coordinates: 32.4260562, -104.2562825
What's to see: After the murder of Eugene Moore in Stringtown in 1932, Bonnie led Clyde and Raymond to her aunt's farmhouse in Carlsbad, New Mexico. Although Elsie Stamps hadn't seen her niece in years, she let the group stay, but Clyde's erratic driving caught the sheriff's attention.

Recognizing that the car they were driving was stolen, the sheriff sought them at the house for questioning. Clyde, Raymond and Bonnie kidnapped the officer instead, driving him all the way to San Antonio. Aunt Elsie alerted authorities right away but remained fearful all of her life that Clyde Barrow would return to kill her. Upon learning that Bonnie had been gunned down in Louisiana, she proclaimed that the girl was probably burning in hell.

Sadly, the house was torn down in 2006, and an empty lot is all that remains of the farm.[168]

72.Bonnie Parker's aunt, whom the gangsters visited with Raymond Hamilton after the Stringtown murder, lived in this house. The aunt was relieved that Bonnie had been killed, whom she believed as "surely in hell" (Carlsbad Current- Argus, April 15 2006; Austin American Statesman, May 24 1934).

Lafayette Hotel, New Orleans
Location: 600 St. Charles Avenue, New Orleans, Louisiana.
Coordinates: 29.9477189, -90.0731639
What's to see: After being freed from Eastham Prison, Raymond Hamilton and Clyde Barrow formed the second iteration of the Barrow Gang. However, their relationship quickly soured after a dispute about how to divvy up their gains from the bank robbery in Lancaster. Raymond left the gang and headed south. In April of 1934, he wrote a letter to the Dallas city attorney on stationary from the Lafayette Hotel in New Orleans, where he claimed he was staying. In this letter, he explained that he had been separated from Clyde "since the Lancaster bank robbery" to indicate that he had no culpability in the murder of Cal Campbell in Commerce. He even claimed to be "a lone man and intend to stay that way." Raymond didn't stay lone for very long. He was arrested on April 25, 1934, an event that Clyde Barrow commemorated with his own letter, in which he hoped Raymond would fry in the electric chair.

Whiskey Pete's Hotel and Casino

Location: 100 West Primm Boulevard, Jean, Nevada.
Coordinates: 35.6117302, -115.3946468
What's to see: Towards the back of a casino amid a smokey haze is one the largest collections and most macabre of Bonnie and Clyde artifacts. On display are the shirt Clyde wore on the day of his death his sunglasses, and some of Bonnie's personal effects. The exhibit centers around the "Bonnie and Clyde Death Car," a Ford V-8 Deluxe Sedan that is supposedly the authentic car from the deadly Louisiana ambush. The Warrens from Kansas, original owners of the car, leased the car to side-show exhibitors in the years following the sensational shoot-out. Eventually, the car was procured for $250,000 by the casino in 1988.[169]

Many a car has been exhibited, and many a doubt cast, concerning the authentic Bonnie and Clyde "death car." In the 1930s, enterprising carnival operators purposefully shot up their own Fords to make money from exhibitions, leaving definite questions as to authenticity for any vehicle claiming to be the original one. Also, contemporary eye-witnesses described the car as being "sandy" or "tan" in color, while the one on display at Primm appears to be gray.

The Ford exhibited at Primm is not actually gray, however; it is a dull, taupe color. Further, the bullet marks on the driver's side door appear to match those on the photos taken after the car was towed to Arcadia on May 23, 1934. Part of the front windshield seems to have been replaced, indicating the obvious wear and tear that this car would have experienced. It appears that this display is genuine.

73. Bonnie's personal items, such as a hand mirror and a beaded necklace, are also on exhibit (photo by author).

74. The "death car" on display inside a smokey, loud casino in Nevada sits behind plexiglass (photo by author).

75. Clyde's blue "death shirt" was recovered by the casino. The slits in the arms were made by the coroner and his assistants on May 23, 1934 (photo by author).

Epilogue

The exploits of Clyde Barrow and his various accomplices are fairly easy to research. Being in constant trouble with the law allowed Clyde's life to be chronicled very thoroughly — the proliferation of arrest warrants, police reports, trial transcripts, arraignment photographs, wanted posters, FBI files, and newspaper articles that Clyde left in his wake help to weave his history. Anecdotes from family members, acquaintances, gang members, and law enforcement officers, coupled with handy city directories, tax and deed records, help to fill in the gaps of time in his narrative. One could venture to say that Clyde Barrow's life was akin to an open book.

Yet, there's something of an enigma that surrounds Clyde Barrow and his girlfriend Bonnie Parker. They were two kids trapped in a horrendous economic depression with, apparently, no way out. Their parents barely made meager livings without much hope for improvement. The place where Bonnie and Clyde grew up, West Dallas, was an embarrassing bane to a city that prided itself on its progressive outlook. Even if Clyde and Bonnie had done nothing wrong, they lived under suspicion of the law, where lightly veiled hints of harassment and imprisonment became a constant threat merely because of who they were and where they lived.

But they could have "gone straight." They could have accepted living mediocre but respectable lives like their siblings, such as Clyde's sisters Artie and Nell or Bonnie's brother Buster. For some reason, though, Bonnie and Clyde decided early on that they were going to live on the edge and die that way. They had forgiving families, street smarts, few scruples, and a desire to buck the system. Were they destined to become who they ended up being?

Fame has a consistent dark undercurrent. To court fame and notoriety, one must delve into the dark recesses of human nature, venture into seedy alley ways, deal with shady characters, and often debase one's values — all to get ahead. Sometimes, this walk on the dark side pays off, and fortune is the rewards. Many more times, however, the walk leads straight into the abyss, where death and destruction await. Like Bonnie wrote, that kind of road gets dimmer and dimmer, so that one can hardly see where it's going, although everyone knows where it will end.

This book retraces that road. Luckily for us, that road is now a lighted path, where history, mythology, geography, and destiny intertwine.

Resources and Bibliography

Books and Articles Sourced and Recommended about Bonnie and Clyde

Ambush: The Real Story of Bonnie and Clyde by Ted Hinton as told to Larry Grove (Dallas: Southwestern Historical Publications, 1979).
> This retelling of the stakeout, and eventual ambush, of Clyde Barrow and Bonnie Parker is controversial, but offers wonderful insights into the way law enforcement worked in the 1930s.

Assignment Huntsville: Memoirs of a Texas Prison Official by Lee Simmons (Austin: University of Texas Press, 1957).
> Simmons' book was one of the first to expose the Methvin family's culpability in the Bonnie and Clyde ambush, and offers an insider look at the Eastham State Prison Farm Raid (or "rescue," as Emma Parker put it).

Bonnie and Clyde: A Twenty-First Century Update by James R. Knight with Jonathan Davis (Austin: Eakin Press, 2003).
> This book is an excellent, easy-to-read, foot-noted, well researched compendium on Bonnie and Clyde, with many never-before seen photographs and new stories uncovered. The authors also devote space to the Bonnie and Clyde harboring trial, which other chroniclers have overlooked.

I'm Frank Hamer: The Life of a Texas Peace Officer by John H. Jenkins and H. Gordon Frost (Austin: State House Press, 1968).
> A grandiose retelling of Frank Hamer's life, this biography paints Hamer in an almost saintly light. The stories in this book aren't always the most reliable, however.

My Life with Bonnie and Clyde by Blanche Caldwell Barrow, edited by John Neal Phillips (Norman: University of Oklahoma Press, 2004).
> Blanche Barrow's memoirs add an entirely new — and often juicier — perspective on Bonnie and Clyde. Extensively foot-noted, this book is a great read.

On the Trail of Bonnie and Clyde: Then and Now by Winston G. Ramsey (Essex: After the Battle, 2003).
> The author, an English Bonnie and Clyde aficionado, goes back to the places where Bonnie and Clyde hid out and chronicles the locations. A

great snapshot of how the American historical and geographical landscapes have changed, this is not a travelogue but a pictorial reenactment of the Barrow Gang. (Note: After the Battle Publications is an excellent resource of then/now books, many of which focus on battle fields of World War II).

"Riding with Bonnie and Clyde: The Real-Life Model for C.W. Moss tells it like it was." W.D. Jones. Playboy Magazine, November 1968, 151, 160-165.
> W.D. Jones wrote about his time with Bonnie and Clyde in a folksy, engaging style.

Running with Bonnie and Clyde: The Ten Fast Years of Ralph Fults by John Neal Phillips (Norman: University of Oklahoma Press, 1996).
> Considered an authoritative work on Bonnie and Clyde, Phillips delved into the history of the Barrow gang by interviewing a former gang member.

The Lives and Times of Bonnie and Clyde by E.R. Milner (Carbondale, Illinois: Southern Illinois University Press, 1996).
> Milner, a professor of history, offers a more intellectual treatment of the crime duo.

The True Story of Bonnie and Clyde as Told by Bonnie's Mother and Clyde's Sister, Mrs. Emma Parker and Mrs. Nell Barrow Cowan (former title: Fugitives) by Jan Fortune (New York: Signet Books, 1968.)
> This true-crime genre book is the first book most Bonnie and Clyde researchers use, though there are some errors, and some names were changed/omitted to protect the not-so-innocent.

The Strange History of Bonnie and Clyde by John Treherne (New York: Cooper Square Press, 1984).
> A psychological study of the weirdness that was Bonnie and Clyde's relationship, this book is more conversational than it is academic.

Recommended and Sourced Websites

Frank Ballinger's Texas Hideout:
http://texashideout.tripod.com/bc.htm
> Ballinger's site is incredibly detailed and is constantly updated with new information, including excerpts from original newspaper articles about the gang, vintage photographs, and family histories. This website is a must-read for any Bonnie and Clyde searcher.

Henry Methvin:
http://www.tmethvin.com/henry
> This site is an excellent and well-documented account of Henry Methvin's life and crimes, with plenty of photos, primary sources, and links.

Blanche Caldwell Barrow:
http://blanchebarrow.com
> Deborah Moss, Blanche's cousin, authored a fun and respectful site for Blanche Barrow, with photos, memoires, resources, and really great music.

Museums and Such

Bonnie and Clyde Ambush Museum
Admission charged, free parking, buses welcome.
2419 Main Street
Gibsland, Louisiana 71028
318-843-1934
http://bonnieandclydemuseum.com

Collingsworth County Museum
Free admission, free parking.
PO Box 495, Wellington, TX 79095
806-447-5327
http://www.collingsworthcountymuseum.org/news.htm

Fort Worth Stockyards National Historical District
Free admission to Stockyards, parking fees, admissions fees where applicable.
Exchange Avenue and Main Street
Fort Worth, Texas 76164
817-626-7921

http://www.fortworthstockyards.org/

Joplin Mining Museum
Admission charged, free parking.
504 S Schifferdecker Ave
Joplin, Missouri 64801
417-623-1180

Old Red Courthouse Museum
Admission charged, parking fees.
100 South Houston St.
Dallas, TX 75202
214-745-1100
http://www.oldred.org/

Texas Prison Museum
Admission charged, free parking.
491 SH 75 North
Huntsville, Texas 77320
http://www.txprisonmuseum.org/

Texas Ranger Museum and Hall of Fame
Admission charged, free parking.
100 Texas Ranger Trail
Waco, Texas 76706
254-750-8631
http://www.texasranger.org/

Cities and Such

Arcadia, Louisiana Official Webpage: http://www.arcadialouisiana.org
Dallas, Texas Convention and Visitor's Bureau:
    http://www.visitdallas.com/visitors
Denton, Texas Visitor's Guide:
    http://www.discoverdenton.com
Dexter, Iowa Community Website:
    http://www.dexteriowa.org
Fort Worth, Texas Visitor's Bureau:
    http://www.fortworth.com
Grapevine, Texas Convention and Visitor's Bureau:
    http://www.grapevinetexasusa.com

Joplin, Missouri Convention and Visitor's Bureau:
    http://www.joplincvb.com
Kansas City, Missouri Convention and Visitor's Bureau:
    http://www.visitkc.com
Kaufman, Texas Official City Website:
    http://www.kaufmantx.org
Lancaster, Texas Chamber of Commerce:
    http://www.lancastertx.org
Platte City, Missouri Official Website:
    http://www.plattecity.org
Shreveport, Louisiana Visitor's Guide:
    http://www.shreveport-bossier.org
Waco, Texas Convention and Visitor's Bureau:
    http://www.wacocvb.com

Index

Alcorn, Bob 20,42,50,55,56(img),100
Alabama Bend, Louisiana 56,94
Alma, Arkansas 5 (list),9,38(img),102,106,109,137 (n),141 (n)
Arbuckle Mountains 118
Amarillo, Texas 45
Arcadia, Louisiana 55,56,60,61,64,65,85,94,95,100,101,127
Arlington Baptist College 5 (list),89,97(img)
Arlington Downs 89
Arlington, Texas 89
Bankhead Highway 89,90
Barrow, Artie 122
Barrow, Blanche Caldwell 4(list), 18,20,2325,29,31,32(img),35,37-40(img),
    41(img),68,81,104,106,108,109.115,124,126,135(n),135(n),138(n)
Barrow, Buck 4(list),16,18,23,25,31,32(img),33,37,40(img),41,42,62,68,
    80,86,104,106-109,115,117,
Barrow, Cumie 15,25,31,49,62,68,73,74,78,80,94,95,109
Barrow, Henry 15-17,22,61,62,68,73
Barrow, Nell 15,16,122,125,134(n)
Beatty, Warren 11,71,81
Bienville Parish 54-57(img),67,98,100
Black Lake Bayou, Louisiana 4(list),58,59(img),94,140(n)
Bonnie and Clyde (movie), 11,81
Boyd, Percy 51,52,111
Brennan, David 25
Broaddus, Texas 17
Bucher, John 26,30,53,114,115,135(n)
Bybee, Hilton 44,45,137(n)
Campbell, Cal 8,9,51,55,69,94,110-112,119
Campbell, Jim 8
Captain Joe Bird Cemetery 5(list),114(img),115
Carlsbad, New Mexico 6(list),27,118(img)
Cartwright, Alonzo 57
Cedar Hill, Texas 87,92
Cedar Lawn Public School 16,17(img),75
Cement City, Dallas, Texas 10,12(img),19(img),72-76,78
Chambless, Odell 17,31,63,91,92
Clausse, Frank 16
Commerce, Oklahoma 51,103,110,111,119,128
Conger's Furniture Store 100
Corry, George 37
Costner, Kevin 81
Cowan, Luther 16
Crandall, Texas 82,85
Crown Hill Memorial Park 62,68,72,74,78
Crowson, Major H. 9,44,52,53,55,115,138(n)
Davis, Malcolm 9,31,73,92,102
Death Car 6(list),60,67,116,120
Denton, Texas (city and county) 18,21,52,81,82,85,86,92,127
Deep Ellum 14

Devil's Back Porch 14,72,76,88
Dexfield Park 41,107-109
Dexter, Iowa 5(list),39,41(img),41,102,107(img),108,127
Dillinger, John 10
Dixie-Overland Highway 95
Dove Road 48,87,92
Dunaway, Faye 71,81
Eagle Ford 5(list),14,16,17(img),20,24,73-75,89
Eagle Ford Road 17,24,73,75,89,135(n)
East Dallas 72
Eastham State Prison Farm 22-24,43,44,50,53,54,62,67,68,96,109,110,114-116,119,124,137(n)
Electra, Texas 24
Enid, Oklahoma 38
Erick, Oklahoma 37
Farris, Maggie 31
Ferguson, Miriam 49,50
Fish Trap Cemetery 62,72,74,79,86
Floyd, "Pretty Boy" 38,136(n)
French, Aubrey 44
Fort Richardson 115
Fort Smith, Arkansas 37,38(img),39,106,108
Fort Worth Pike 42(img),76(img),89,140(n)
Fort Worth, Texas 86,89,90,126
Fort Worth Stockyards 87,90(img),126
Fults, Ralph 22,23,24,26,45,81,87,103,125,135(n),138(n)
Gault, Manny 50,555,56(img),81,99(img),100,139(n)
Gibsland, Louisiana 52,57,60,69,85,95,98,126,139(n)
Grand Prairie, Texas 4(list),5(list),26,42(img),88,89,138(n),140(n)
Grapevine, Texas 4(list),5(list),9,31,48,49(img),50,53,75,76,87
Hall, Howard 9,27,83,86,135(n),
Hamer, Frank 50,54-56(img),57,58,61,67,69,81,99(img),100,124,139(n),140(n)
Hamilton, Floyd 17,23,30,31,43,49,63
Hamilton, Raymond 4(list),17,22(img),23,26,27,43-45(img),48,52-54,63,67,73,78,81,82,86,88, 92,93,96,103,110,114-116,119,136(n),138(n)
Harboring Trial 4(list),62(img),68,78,124
Hardy, Paul 37
Harrelson, Woody 81
Harryman, Claude 8
Harryman, Wes 5,9,104,132
Highland Park, Texas 13
Hillsboro, Texas 9,26,30,55
Hinton, Ted 20,50,55,56(img),59,60,100,124,134(n),138(n),139(n)
Howe, Texas 52
Humphrey, Henry 9,38
Huntsville, Texas 5,9,22,25,43,53,57,63,67,96,113-115,124,127
Irving, Texas 48,75,76,88,89
James, Jesse 10,16,46,135(n)
Jean, Nevada 120
Jefferson, Blind Lemon 14
Jefferson, Texas 95

Johnson, Doyle 9,27
Jones, William Deacon (W.D.) 4(list),17,26(img),27,29,30-33,37-41,46,63,67,81,84,102,
    104,106,108,116,117,125,135(n),136(n),137(n),138(n)
Joplin Mining Museum 105,127
Joplin, Missouri 5(list),8,9,31-33,45,52,63,102,104,105(img),127,128
Jordan, Henderson 54-56,58,100
Kansas City, Missouri 47,108,128
Kemp, Texas 5(list),25,87(img)
King's Daughter's Hospital 104,108
Ku Klux Klan 14,90
Lake Dallas 85,93,104
La Reunion 27,74
Lancaster, Texas 5(list),45,27,87,88,88,119,128
Lawrence, Kansas 102,103,140(n)
Ledbetter, Huddie 97
Lewisville Lake 85
Lewisville, Texas 5(list),32,85,87,92,93(img)
Longview, Texas 30(img),94
Lucerne, Indiana 102
Maxwell, C.G. 27
McBride, Lillian 30,31,63,92
McCormick, A.F. 24
McGinnis, Harry 9,32,104
McKamy-Campbell Funeral Home 61
NcNabb, Wade 45,96
Mabank, Texas 25,83,87
Majestic Café 93,97
Maypearl, Texas 82,83
Methvin, Henry 4(list),22,44(img),45(img),46,48,52,53,55-58,63,69,81,92,94,
    98,110-112,116,124,126,139(n)
Methvin, Ivy 44,56,57,94,100,139(n)
Miami, Oklahoma 55,94,110,11(img)
Middleton, Ohio 22
Moore, Eugene 9,27,103,118
Moss, C.W. 46,81,83,125
Mount Lebanon, Louisiana 4(list),57,58(img),59,85,95,98
Muckelroy, Jim 139(n)
Mulligan, Everett 26,103
Mullins, James 43,44
Murphy, H.D. 9,48,49,55,92
Oak Cliff, Texas 13,62
Oakley, Prentiss 55,58,100
O'Dare, Mary 45,52,63,138(n)
Oronogo, Missouri 5(list),27,102,103(img),104
Owens, W.N. 24
Palmer, Joe 22,43-45,52,53,67,96,110,114,115,138(n)
Parker, Charles 19
Parker, Billie 19,37,38,41,49,61,62,68,79,106
Parker, Buster 19,61,79,122,135(n)
Parker, Emma 19,21,37,39,42,61,62,68,72,78,79,86,124,125,137(n),138(n),140(n)
Parsons, Estelle 71

Penn, Arthur 11,25,81
Perry, Iowa 108,109
Phares, S.G. 50,67
Phillips, John Neal 24,43,68,124,125,138(n),139(n)
Platte City, Missouri 38,41,102,107-109,128
Playboy Magazine 29,68,125
Pilot Point, Texas 5(img),82,84(img)
Pollard, Michael 71
Ponder, Texas 5(list),82(img)
Poteau, Oklahoma 5(list),102,110(img)
Primm Valley, Nevada 27,120
Pritchard family and farm 37,116
Red Crown Tourist Court 38,41,107,108
Redfield, Iowa 39,107,108
Red Oak, Texas 4(list),82,83,84(img)
Rembrandt, Iowa 102,109,110
Ringgold, Louisiana 56,59
Rogers, Ted 26,136(n)
Royko, Mike 8
Rowena, Texas 19
R.P. Henry Bank 88
Ruston, Louisiana 37,94
Sailes, Louisiana 4(list),53,56,58(img),94,95,98,140(n)
Salt Fork of the Red River 5(list),16,37
San Augustine, Texas 17
Satanta 115
Scatter gun 30,44
Schifferdecker Park 105
Schmidt, Smoot 20,88,137(n)
Sherman, Jack 25,136(n)
Sherman, Texas 9,27,83,86,135(n)
Shreveport, Louisiana 5(list),54,55,61,67,94,95(img),96(img),97,98,128,139(n),140(n),141(n)
Simmons, Lee 45,50,57,61,67,124,137(n),138(n),139(n)
Smith, Bessie 14
Sowers, Texas 42,76(img),87-89,138(n),140(n)
Stamps, Elsie 118,119
St. Paul's Bottom 95-97
Stuart, Iowa 5(list),70(img),102,103,112(img)
Stringtown, Oklahoma 26,27,102,103,118,119
Swiss Circle Street Car Stop 77
Taylor, James. T.24
Telico Plains, Texas 15
Temple, Texas 9,27
Texarkana Texas and Arkansas, 94
Texas Prison Museum 5(list),67,113(img),114,127
Texas Ranger Museum 116,127
Texas Street 95(img),96,97
The Highway Men (movie) 81
Thornton, Betty 25
Thornton, Roy 20,21,68,78

Topeka, Kansas 52,66,67
Top of the Hill Terrace 89(img),90
U.S. 80 5(list),42,89,90,94,95(img),140(n)
Van Buren, Arkansas 102,106
Venus, Texas 5(list),82,83(img)
Waco, Texas 18,21,24,29,67,113,116,128
Wade, J.L. 60
Wall's Unit 22,23.67,115
Warren, Ruth and Jesse 52,66,67,120
Warren Wagon Train 115
Waskom, Texas 45,94,96
Wellington, Texas 37,106,113,116,117,126
West Dallas 4(list),12(img),15(img),16,17(img),18-20,23-26,29-31,42,43,48, 50,62,68,72-76,81,92,102,122,135(n)
Western Heights Cemetery 62,68,72,80
Wheeler, E.B. 9,48,55,92
Whiskey Pete's Casino 67,120
Wilder, Gene 71
Williams, Eleanor 17,135(n)
Yost, Fred 43

Shameless Self Promotional Page

For the Road Tripper who doesn't have everything just yet…. Check out the other titles in the Traveling History series!

Traveling History Up the Cattle Trails: A Road Tripper's Guide to the Cattle Roads of the Southwest

Traveling History Amongst the Ghosts: A Road Tripper's Guide to Ghost Towns in the Red River Valley

The Stark Ranch of Cooke County, Texas: History that spans the Red River

Traveling History with Bonnie and Clyde: A Road Tripper's Guide to Gangster (and Gangster Movie) Sites in in the Southwest

Traveling History of the John F. Kennedy Assassination: The Routes and Sites of November 22, 1963 (forthcoming July 2022)

Red River Historian Press
robin@redriverhistorian.com

To book presentations, inquire about consulting services, join a tour, and browse the store to order the Traveling History Guides — or just to discover more stories, photos, and maps — visit

https://www.redriverhistorian.com

[1] The Trinity River was unpredictable – both in 1906 and 1908, the river flooded so badly that West Dallas was cut off from the rest of the city for months as several bridges washed away. Throughout the 20th century, large engineering projects straightened out the river channel through a series of levees, but the Trinity still floods from time to time.

[2] Today's West Dallas is still an economically depressed area, though it's home to more Hispanics and African Americans than Southern whites. When the area was incorporated in 1952, Dallas renamed many of the streets to celebrate the city's movers and shakers, with the effect that West Dallas lost some of its distinctiveness. For example, Eagle Ford Road, named after one of the earliest settlements in Dallas County and the street on which Clyde lived, was renamed Singleton Boulevard in honor of Dallas County Commissioner Vernon Singleton.

[3] In Dallas, street bridges over the Trinity River were labeled as "viaducts."

[4] Jan I. Fortune, ed., True Story of Bonnie and Clyde as told by Bonnie's Mother and Clyde's Sister, Mrs. Emma Parker and Mrs. Nell Barrow Cowan (New York: Signet Books, 1968), 30-39.

[5] In Fortune's book, Clyde's sister Nell names the school "Cedar Valley."

[6] Dime-store novels were mass-marketed, short novellas that were often serialized. Topics ranged from mysteries to romances to westerns. These books introduced mythologies about historical characters that are sometimes still believed, such as the idea that Jesse James "robbed from the rich and gave to the poor." Historians who focus on the U.S. West and U.S. South have had to dispel much of the fabrications that these paperbacks printed, as some of the fictionalization has made it into school textbooks and still continue to cloud the facts.

[7] Dallas city directories; John Neal Phillips, Running with Bonnie and Clyde: The Ten Fast Years of Ralph Fults (Norman, Oklahoma: University of Oklahoma Press, 1996), 44. Some sources explain that the Barrows moved their little house from far west Dallas on Rural Route 6 to the Star Service Station.

[8] Dallas city directories.

[9] Fortune, 32. Phillips, 45-46. In her recollections, Nell calls Eleanor "Anne."

[10] Fortune, 32-33. The rental car agency dropped the theft charges against Clyde after retrieving the car intact.

[11] Fortune, 36-41.

[12] Ibid, 43. Dallas city directories.

[13] Dallas Public Library, Cement City Collection.

[14] Ibid

[15] Fortune, 47.

[16] Fortune, 42; W.D. Jones, "Riding with Bonnie and Clyde." Playboy Magazine, November 1968, 162.

[17] Fortune, 49.

[18] Blanche Caldwell Barrow and John Neal Phillips, ed. My Life with Bonnie and Clyde (Norman, Oklahoma: University of Oklahoma Press, 2004), 25.

[19] Fortune, 48.

[20] Ibid, 49.

[21] Ibid.

[22] Ted Hinton. Ambush: The Real Story of Bonnie and Clyde (Dallas: Southwestern Historical Publications, 1979), 7-8, 113-114. Ted Hinton writes that he met Bonnie at the American Café in 1930.

[23] Fortune, 57. In Bonnie and Clyde: A Twentieth Century Update, James R. Knight writes that Clyde and his friend, Clarence Clay, visited Buster Parker's (Bonnie's brother) house, where Bonnie and several other people had gathered for some relaxed conversation and visiting (23). According to Phillips, Bonnie was simply visiting her friend (47). The Clays were kin to the Parkers.
[24] Ibid, 58-67.
[25] Ibid, 69-76.
[26] Along with hardened criminals, Eastham's population consisted of first time offenders, juveniles, and many poor (and mostly black) men who had been caught "loitering," which could earn them a year's sentence in the segregated South. This cruel system is a product of the 13th amendment's caveat, which excepts slavery and involuntary servitude "as punishment for crime whereof the party shall have been duly convicted" (U.S. Constitution, amend. 1865). For more on the decidedly cruel Texas prison system, and subsequent reforms, read Penology for Profit by Donald R. Walker.
[27] Phillips, 49-54.
[28] Fortune, 76-78.
[29] Phillips, 54.
[30] Ibid, 65.
[31] Fort Worth Star Telegram, December 18 1932.
[32] Ibid, 49-54.
[33] Fortune, 85.
[34] Phillips' Running with Bonnie and Clyde references a bank robbery by the Barrow gang in Lawrence, Kansas that netted them $33,000 during this early gang period. No other historical account, neither in newspapers or police reports, has included this robbery.
[35] Other accounts maintain that Raymond Hamilton was instrumental in planning the future Eastham Raid. While Raymond had been reluctant to commit armed robbery, he ended up being the gang member with the most bank jobs to his name, although Clyde was implicated in a good number of them.
[36] Corsicana Daily Sun, April 14 1932. Phillips, 75-78.
[37] Dallas Morning News, April 21, 1932; Fortune, 81-83. Phillips, 89-101.
[38] Dallas Morning News, April 21, 1932.
[39] Phillips, 101.
[40] Caldwell Barrow, 193.
[41] Fortune, 89.
[42] Phillips, 74.
[43] Ted Rogers, a one-time member of the Barrow Gang, later bragged about his role in the killing to fellow cell mates. He was never charged with the crime. Raymond Hamilton received the death penalty for Bucher's murder, though he maintained that he was in Michigan at that time. Fort Worth Star Telegram, December 18 1932.
[44] Corsicana Daily Sun, August 6 1932; Kilgore News Herald, August 8 1932.
[45] This murder occurred at S. R. Little Grocery, 624 S. Vaden Street. The building no longer stands. Clyde's and/or Raymond's guilt in Howard Hall's murder is still open for debate. Raymond Hamilton was captured in Bay City, Michigan shortly afterwards, but he maintained that he wasn't there – and neither was Clyde. The Sherman Police pinned the crime on Clyde Barrow without an investigation, anyway. The Whitewright Sun, October 13 1932; Fort Worth Star Telegram, December 7 1932.
[46] Austin American, December 26 1932. In latter reports, W.D. Jones was sometimes mistaken for "Pretty Boy" Floyd, another notorious criminal from the Southwest, or Bob Brady, an escaped murderer from the penitentiary in McAlester, Oklahoma. Jones used many aliases: "Hubert Bleigh." "Herbert Bly," and "Jack Sherman."

47 Fortune, 89.
48 Carlsbad Current Argus, August 17 1932.
49 ibid
50 The Marshall News Messenger, April 25 1932.
51 Lee Simmons, Assignment Huntsville (Austin: University of Texas Press, 1957), 128.
52 Phillips, 160.
53 Frank Ballinger, Texas Hideout http://texashideout.tripod.com/bc.htm.
54 Waco News-Tribune, December 8 1932.
55 W.D. Jones statement to Dallas Police, November 1933, Dallas Municipal Archives.
56 Fortune, 107-109; Tyler Courier Times, January 8 1933.
57 Fortune, 109-112.
58 Ibid, 112.
59 Ibid, 113.
60 Sedalia Democrat, April 14 1933.
61 Blanche had always criticized the movie, in which she was depicted as running hysterically into the middle of the melee. In her memoirs, she maintained that she was quite calm. She also wrote that, unlike in the movie, Bonnie never shot at the officers (Caldwell Barrow, 36). W.D. Jones later told interviewers that Bonnie would reload, but would not shoot, though Emma Parker relayed that Bonnie did shoot when needed.
62 Fortune, 83-85.
63 Caldwell Barrow, 81-87. According to W.D. Jones's statement with the Dallas police in November 1933, he had left Bonnie and Clyde and returned to Dallas. He rejoined them a few weeks later.
64 Fortune, 123. Texas State Historical Marker, Collingsworth County.
65 Ibid, 124.
66 Ibid, 124.
67 Wellington Leader, June 15 1933.
68 W.D. Jones Statement, November 16, 1933, Vertical Files, Dallas Public Library. Simmons, 122.
69 Fortune, 127-128; Caldwell, 110-117.
70 Phillips, Texas Hideout
71 Caldwell Barrow, 100-110; Fortune, 131.
72 Kansas City Times, August 3 1933. Buck Barrow and W.D. Jones were accused of having robbed the Commercial Bank in Alma, Arkansas and during the robbery, tied up Marshal Henry Humphries. However, the pair were in Fayetteville, casing the grocery stores there. After absconding with money stolen from the Brown Grocery, the men were cornered by Marshal Henry Humphries, whom Buck Barrow shot. Humphries died from his wounds a few days later.
73 Fortune, 129.
74 Ibid, 132.
75 Caldwell Barrow, 100-110.
76 Kansas City Times, July 20 1933.
77 Fortune, 134. Caldwell Barrow, 116-117.
78 Fortune, 135; Caldwell Barrow, 121; Kansas City Star, July 25 1933.
79 Sioux City Journal, July 28 1933.
80 Fortune, 135.
81 Fortune, 136-137; Caldwell Barrow, 126-127; The Courier (Waterloo, IA) July 24 1933.
82 Fortune, 135-142.
83 Dallas Morning News, July 24, 1933. Caldwell Barrow, 133-134.
84 Kansas City Star, July 25 1933.

[85] Caldwell Barrow, 178-179; 184-187. Blanche Barrow Official Site, http://www.blanchebarrow.com
[86] W.D. Jones Statement; Phillips, 151; The Times (Shreveport), November 26 1933.
[87] Fortune, 146.
[88] St. Louis Post-Dispatch, May 24 1934.
[89] Marshall News Messenger, November 23 1933; Fort Worth Star Telegram, November 23, 1933.
[90] Ibid, 149-152. Emma Parker related that the family reunion occurred in Wise County, Texas, but contemporary newspaper accounts locate the failed ambush north of Grand Prairie, near the now-defunct town of Sowers on Sowers Road (today's Pioneer Parkway). Since Sheriff Smoot Schmid had no authority in any county but Dallas, one must surmise that Emma Parker was mistaken.
[91] Simmons, 125.
[92] Fortune, 155. John Neal Phillips writes that Hilton Bybee was added to the raid by Ralph Fults, not Raymond Hamilton, and Lee Simmons related that Bybee was a "hanger on" and wasn't part of the original escape plan.
[93] According to John Neal Phillips, Joe Palmer had set his sights on Crowson due to a beating he had received by him, though Ted Hinton maintained in his book that Crowson was a decent man. Lee Simmons wrote that Major Crowson's assignment as a mounted guard was to stay well beyond the work detail area so that the prisoners never knew exactly where he was. That morning, however, Major Crowson rode up to talk to the work detail guards, which ended up costing him his life.
[94] Corsicana Daily Sun, January 16 1934.
[95] Tyler Morning Telegraph, April 26 1934.
[96] Emma Parker maintained that Joe Palmer stayed with Bonnie and Clyde up until the Grapevine murders (Fortune, True Story of Bonnie and Clyde).
[97] Simmons, 166.
[98] Fortune, 158. Many of Mary's more unfortunate characteristics, such as hysterics and loose sexual morals, have been attributed to both Bonnie and Blanche in books and movies.
[99] Fortune, 158; Dallas Morning News, May 23, 1934. Emma Parker and Nell Barrow Cowan doubted that this letter was genuine, though the newspaper claimed a thumb print on the letter matched Barrow's.
[100] The "kidnap demand" refers to the kidnapping of an oil tycoon by George Kelly, known as "Machine Gun Kelly." The "Kansas City Depot job" refers to the June 1933 ambush of police officers transferring a criminal by Chester Floyd, called "Pretty Boy Floyd" in the newspapers. Both criminals have southwestern connections: Machine Gun Kelly's family lived in Wise County, Texas (he's buried in Paradise, Texas after serving a life imprisonment due to the kidnapping) and Floyd grew up in Oklahoma. 1933 proved a terrible year of crime due to exploits by Kelly, Floyd, and "Public Enemy Number One," John Dillinger. However, 1934 became a banner year for law enforcement with the deaths of Bonnie and Clyde (May 1934), John Dillinger (July 1934), Pretty Boy Floyd (October 1934), and the arrest and conviction of Machine Gun Kelly.
[101] Fortune, 160-161.
[102] Fort Worth Star Telegram, April 2 1934.
[103] Fort Worth Star Telegram, February 24 1935.
[104] Fortune, 161. James R. Knight with Jonathan Davis, Bonnie and Clyde: A Twenty-First Century Update (Austin: Eakin Press, 2003), 145.
[105] Fort Worth Star Telegram, April 2 1934.
[106] Fortune, 149.
[107] Daily News (New York), May 27 1934.

[108] Dallas Morning News, May 24, 1934; Simmons, 128
[109] During this period, Texas law prohibited pursuits across county lines – all law enforcement dealing with crimes beyond their county's jurisdiction would first need special permission to work in another county. Due in part to Clyde's crime spree, Texas changed the law to allow law enforcement more leverage.
[110] Daily News (New York), May 27, 1934. According to wire reports from May 24, 1934 reported in various newspapers, Hamer and Gault logged over 15,000 miles in their pursuit of Clyde Barrow.
[111] Dallas Morning News, May 23, 1934; Fortune, 162-163.
[112] Denton Record-Chronicle, April 7 1934.
[113] Kansas City Star, April 7 1934.
[114] ibid
[115] Bonnie and Clyde Hideout. Phillips, 193.
[116] Phillips, 192.
[117] Dallas Morning News, May 23, 1934. Hinton, 154. Phillips, 193. Fortune, 158.
[118] The family reunion location may have been near Martinsville, Texas. Clyde's uncle on his mother's side, Jim Muckelroy, had a farm near the town, located in Nacogdoches County, and verified to the FBI that Bonnie and Clyde had visited him a couple of times previously. During their first visit to Muckelroy's farm in September 1932, Bonnie accidently shot one of her toes off.
[119] Fortune, 166.
[120] Ibid; Fort Worth Star Telegram, May 23 1934; "Henry Methvin." http://www.tmethvin.com/henry/index.html
[121] Hinton, 158-159. Henry later testified that he purposefully separated from Bonnie and Clyde, which was part of the ambush plan.
[122] Methvin v. Oklahoma (1936).
[123] The Fort Worth Star Telegram reported on May 23, 1934 that the "father of escaped Texas convict put Barrow on spot" but did not mention Ivy Methvin by name.
[124] Oddly, Hamer's account puts this stump/hiding place "eight miles from Plain Dealing, Louisiana," though Plain Dealing is not in such close proximity to Gibsland. Plain Dealing is north of Shreveport, just south of the Arkansas border. John H. Jenkins and H. Gordon Frost. I'm Frank Hamer: The Life of a Texas Peace Officer (Austin State House Press, 1968), 222.
[125] Weekly Town Talk (Alexandria, Louisiana), May 26 1934.
[126] Fort Worth Star Telegram, May 24 1934.
[127] Simmons, 133. It is still unclear if Henry Methvin was aware of this plot or not.
[128] Shreveport Times, May 24, 1934.
[129] Descriptions based on Running with Bonnie and Clyde by John Neal Phillips; Ambush by Ted Hinton, and Bonnie and Clyde Hideout by Frank R. Ballinger.
[130] According to Ted Hinton in Ambush, Clyde was not wearing shades because the sun was behind him. However, in photos of Clyde being brought to the coroner after the ambush, his shades dangle from his ears.
[131] Daily News (New York), May 27 1934. The farmer who claimed to have witnessed the ambush did not share his name. He described a tan car, but the car was actually gray; he also called Ivy Methvin "Irvin" even though his given name was Ivy.
[132] St. Louis Post-Dispatch, May 24 1934; Fort Worth Star-Telegram, May 24 1934.
[133] Phillips, 310.
[134] Hinton, 169.
[135] Ibid, 170-171.
[136] Daily News (New York), May 27, 1934.

137 Corsicana Semi-Weekly Light, May 25 1934.
138 Fortune, 173-174.
139 Phillips, 209-210.
140 Fortune, 173.
141 Corsicana Semi-Weekly Light, May 25 1934.
142 Fortune, 170. Dallas Times Herald, May 24, 1934.
143 Corsicana Semi-Weekly Light, May 25 1934.
144 Letter on Adolphus Hotel stationary, n.d., DeGoyler Library, Southern Methodist University.
145 Texas Hideout; Dallas Morning News, May 27, 1934; Dallas Morning News, "Hidden History 1926-1950" July 3, 2002.
146 Waco-Tribune Herald, May 27, 1934.
147 Corsicana Semi-Weekly Light, May 29, 1934.
148 Fortune, 174-175.
149 Dallas Morning News, May 23, 1934.
150 Dallas Times Herald, May 24, 1934.
151 Fort Worth Star Telegram, February 23, 1935.
152 Rachel Stone, "History: A lesser told story, the aftermath (and crimes) of those Bonnie and Clyde left behind." Oak Cliff Advocate, September 19, 2016.
153 Because Emma Parker was a renter, she tended to move annually to keep her rent payments within budget. In 1929, she lived on Crockett Street (the Meyerson Center now occupies the site). In 1930, she lived at 1134 Hickory Street near the Cedars neighborhood. She learned of Bonnie's death in the rent house at 232 West 8th Street, which still stands.
154 Hamer claimed in interviews that Bonnie was pregnant at the time of her death, but both the coroner and the undertaker independently refuted this. Bonnie, like many women in the era, may have used Lysol as a form of "feminine deodorant" and birth control, effectively and dangerously sterilizing herself.
155 Some of the locations in Ellis County were also used for other movies based on the Great Depression, such as "Places in the Heart." The buildings and scenery are fairly accurate to the settings, but one glaring mistake in these movies are the electric poles that line the landscape. In rural Texas, electrification was not widely available until the 1960s.
156 According to Emma Parker, "we were parked seventy-five feet from the main highway… we were parked facing away from the pike on the right side of the road" (Fortune, p. 149). The "pike" was the Fort Worth Pike, also known as U.S. 80 as well as Grand Prairie's Main Street (today, U.S. 180). However, the newspapers reported that the ambush occurred eight miles north of Grand Prairie. Some modern histories place the ambush at TX 114 and Sowers Road, but this is not the "pike" that was referred to in the 1930s.
157 The Shreveport Journal, May 24, 1934.
158 Shreveport Journal, May 23, 1934; Fort Worth Star Telegram, May 23, 1934. The Fort Worth Star Telegram placed them at "Black Lake" which is a body of water much further south near Campti in Natchitoches Parish; the newspaper probably meant "Black Lake Bayou" which is just west of Sailes and the ambush site.
159 Shreveport Journal, May 23, 1934.
160 Southern cities favored rezoning majority black neighborhoods into vice districts in order to collect taxes, keep African Americans from moving to other areas of town, and to justify a heavy police presence within their neighborhood. Since most of the land was owned by wealthy whites who collected rents from the shotgun house they crowded together, the Southern elite profited from the talents in these zones while also keeping firm control over the people within the zones. Today, the Shreveport Police Department maintains a strong

presence in this area, as they built their headquarters in the historically African American neighborhood just to the west of St. Paul's Bottom.

[161] Fortune, 101-102; Jasper County News, December 1, 1932.

[162] The site of the tourist courts was bought by Forest Park Cemetery Perpetual Care, which extended its graveyard to the corner.

[163] The building that once housed Brown Grocery in 1933 has been replaced by a church parking lot.

[164] James R. Knight, "Incident at Alma: The Barrow Gang in Northwest Arkansas." The Arkansas Historical Quarterly 56, 4 (1997), 399-426.

[165] Poteau News, January 25, 1934; Eric Standridge, "A Tale of Bonnie and Clyde: The Bank Robbery at Poteau, Oklahoma." Owlcation.com (June 24, 2021).

[166] Des Moines Tribune, April 16, 1934.

[167] Prior to 1928, individual counties executed inmates sentenced to death, usually by the gallows. After 1928, the death penalty became the state's obligation. Methods of execution have changed from electric chair to gas chamber to lethal injection. The State of Texas has killed more people than any other legal entity in the United States, though Oklahoma has the highest per capita execution rate.

[168] Carlsbad Current-Argus, April 15 2006.

[169] Kansas City Star, Au<u>tomotiv</u>e Market Place advertising section, December 13 2013.

www.ingramcontent.com/pod-product-compliance
Lightning Source LLC
Chambersburg PA
CBHW070045120526
44589CB00035B/2323